CSS *for* Print Designers

JD Graffam

CSS for Print Designers
JD Graffam

New Riders
1249 Eighth Street
Berkeley, CA 94710
510/524-2178
510/524-2221 (fax)

Find us on the Web at: www.newriders.com
To report errors, please send a note to errata@peachpit.com.

New Riders is an imprint of Peachpit, a division of Pearson Education.

Acquisition Editor: Wendy Sharp
Project Editor: Becca Freed
Production Editor: Danielle Foster
Development Editor: Judy Ziajka
Copyeditor: Naomi Adler Dancis
Proofreader: Suzie Nasol
Compositor: Danielle Foster
Indexer: Rebecca Plunkett
Cover design: Aren Howell Straiger
Interior design: Danielle Foster

ISBN-13   978-0-321-76588-8
ISBN-10   0-321-76588-5

9 8 7 6 5 4 3 2 1

Printed and bound in the United States of America

Dedication

I'm renting a cabin near Pickwick Lake, where Tennessee, Mississippi, and Alabama touch. I'm here by myself to finish writing this book—to focus. The cabin is a one-room A-frame with a little back porch that overlooks a deep hollow.

Rather than waking up to the Rock 103 deejays, early morning bird songs get me up. I'm not chasing new business throughout the day; squirrels are chasing each other across the tin roof. And at midnight, instead of police sirens, packs of coyotes yip in the distance.

It's been nice to be alone, focusing on my writing. But today, I need to get out of this cabin and on the water to write. There are two reasons for this.

The first reason is practical: It's March and I need to take half a day to make sure our pontoon boat is ready for the summer season. After a quick wipe-down and a two-minute drive from dry storage to the state park, I put her in the water and turn the key—she fires right up without a problem.

The second reason is to dedicate this book to my family. I cannot think of a more appropriate place to write a dedication to my family than on the water, because the special memories I have with everyone in my family are surrounded by water: Lake D'Arbonne, Lake Claiborne, Lake Travis, and Lake Acworth; the Gulf of Mexico, the Pacific Ocean, and the Atlantic; the Ouachita River, Mississippi River, Red River, Tennessee River, and last, but not least, the Loutre Bottom.

I idle slowly across the choppy water into a cove, drop anchor, and start writing. It's windy. Ten minutes in, the boat is banging up against the shore and tangled in lost fishing line. I adjust, drop anchor again. This time the anchor holds.

I write the dedication: "To family, the single important thing in life."

The wind is picking up—waves are slapping against the rocks on the shore, floating docks are squeaking, and the birds are flying low. A thunderstorm will settle over the lake tonight. But for now, I'm enjoying the water. I'm hundreds of miles away from my family, but I'm connected to them. I fold up my laptop and float.

Acknowledgments

I want to acknowledge these people for their inspiration and for helping make this book possible:

Denise Jacobs, author of The *CSS Detective's Guide*, for introducing me to Peachpit Press. She is the primary reason this book exists.

AIGA chapters and print designers across the country, for letting me lead my CSS for Print Designers workshops.

My Peachpit friends, for sticking with me as I went through the process of writing my first book. I learned a lot, mostly how patient y'all are.

And finally, the wonderful people I work with every day. To my team at Simple Focus, to our clients who trust us to make their Web sites the right way, and to the Memphis design community.

CONTENTS

INTRODUCTION

A while back, I volunteered to lead a CSS workshop in Memphis. I came up with the idea because it seemed like I kept having the same conversation with print designers, especially after a couple rounds of beer at AIGA mixers. The conversations would go something like this:

Me: "This beer is pretty good."

Print Designer: "Yeah, I'm a little buzzed. Geez, I wish I could code Web sites by hand."

Me: "I bet you could learn it pretty quickly. It's easy. I'm buzzed, too."

Print Designer: "No way. My mind just doesn't work like yours. I'm more of a visual kind of person."

Me: "No, seriously—I used to be a print designer. I could show you the basics in a few minutes. Coding is a lot more visual than you might think."

Print Designer: "Yeah, right."

Me: "I'm not kidding."

Print Designer: "You should do a workshop about this, then. I bet it'd do really well. And you should serve beer at it."

After a while, I started thinking a little more about the idea of teaching CSS to print designers. I was convinced that with three hours I could teach CSS to someone who'd never hand-coded before. It would have to be basic. It'd have to move fast. Print designers are pretty tech-savvy people—they can learn this stuff.

So with the help of AIGA Memphis, I organized a workshop. We called it CSS for Print Designers. It sold out after only a few days of promotion, so we organized a second one, which sold out within 48 hours. A few weeks later, I got an email about doing a workshop in a different city. Then I got another email, and another, and another.

I think the timing of this book is perfect. Five years ago there were print designers who didn't touch Web projects, and Web designers who didn't code. Now there's hardly a single print designer who hasn't been asked to design something for the Web, and almost every Web designer knows how to code CSS by hand.

The gap between designer and coder is closing, and fast. There's an entire generation of pixel-native designers coming up. To them, CSS is just another design tool. When you're done reading this book, I want you to feel the same way.

Who This Book Is For

This book covers the basics of how to code Web sites by hand with a plain text editor. It's deliberately short and written in a casual voice, without jargon or geek-speak.

Who should read it?

- A designer or visual thinker who's ready to take the first step toward finally learning how to code by hand

- A designer who has tried to read other books or online tutorials about coding Web sites, but came away overwhelmed and frustrated

- A designer looking for a way to communicate better with coders when handing off projects to them

- An art or design student who wants to make Web sites but isn't interested in a computer science degree

- A design professor who needs to teach students the latest Web standards and technology

What This Book Is Not

This book is not a comprehensive resource. For example, there are over 100 HTML elements, but this book covers only the dozen or so that are used the most and instructs the reader to search for the rest. It doesn't cover everything there is to know about Web design—that's what the Internet is for.

This book is not philosophical. While this book is perfect for students and professors, it does not cover the *why* of code. Instead, it focuses on the *how*. It's just practical like that.

This book is not a workbook. While there are practical examples scattered throughout, this book doesn't start with Chapter 1 and walk you through step-by-step how to build a Web site. Instead, it teaches concepts in a logical order with contextual examples that help explain those concepts.

This book is not for computer novices. Print designers work with specialized software and know all about the Internet, so the readers of this book need to be comfortable working with applications like Photoshop, InDesign, or Illustrator and making their way around online.

1

Coding in Plain English

Coding CSS Is Like Learning the Simplest Language Ever

I TOOK AN embarrassingly high number of Spanish courses over the years (eight in total) for someone who can't speak Spanish very well. While I can read it with a Spanish-to-English dictionary handy, I'm at a loss if asked to come up with it from scratch. If I ever get left behind by a cruise boat in Cancún, I know just enough to find the restroom, hospital, or library.

In the fourth grade I learned what I needed to know—20 or 30 words, some basic syntax, and upside-down question marks. *Hola. Mi nombre es... ¿Donde esta la biblioteca?*

At some point, you'll be handed a change order for a Web site update, and just like me with my Spanish-to-English dictionary, you already know enough (with Google as a resource) to get along, making simple changes to an existing Web site. If you were given font-size: 12px; or width: 200px; you'd easily decipher what it means and how to manipulate it.

CSS Is Easy to Memorize

The most helpful lesson I learned in my Spanish classes was about cognates. A *cognate* is a word that has a similar meaning (and usually looks or sounds similar) across multiple languages, such as *education* in English and *educacíon* in Spanish. That lesson helped me to see a lot of similarities between Spanish and English: We're saying the same thing, just with slightly different words and some funny characters sprinkled throughout. If you're just reading another language, memorizing cognates is often unnecessary because they already look like words you know.

Check out TABLE 1.1, which breaks down some common CSS into plain English:

TABLE 1.1 CSS–Typography Cognates

CSS	ENGLISH
font-size	The size of the font
color	The color of something
height	The height of something
letter-spacing	Kerning (the horizontal space between letters)
line-height	Leading (the vertical space taken up by a line of text)

See? This stuff's easy. Way easier than a real language, in fact, because there are fewer vocabulary terms in total—and no verb conjugations.

You Already Know How to Read CSS

Let's take a look at what some real CSS looks like. For now, I don't want you to worry about the funny characters, or the spaces, or the formatting, or anything else that's confusing or intimidating. Those are just CSS's version of upside-down question marks. All they do is tell you what to expect next, and they don't change the meaning. Just read it like it's plain English.

```
.mexican-restaurant{
  font-family: georgia;
  font-size: 16px;
  background-image: url(margarita.gif);
  background-color: lime;
  }
```

A noncoder could easily describe how this code would render in plain English: Something like, "This thing called Mexican Restaurant uses the Georgia typeface set at 16 pixels. There'd be a graphic of a margarita on a lime-colored background."

We'll take a closer look at this code later. For now, just relax a little, knowing how easy it is to pick apart CSS. You can read code like it's plain English, even if you can't write it from scratch.

2

From Picas to Pixels

Learning and Embracing the Medium of the Internet

WE PRINT DESIGNERS are the type of people who like to turn things over in our hands and see them from all angles. We care about paper selection for the way it feels and how the ink will react. We run our fingers down the binding. We ensure that our most important jobs have a press check in the budget. And when we're out to dinner with our families, they roll their eyes when we drag our fingernails across the varnish of the menu to see if it leaves a mark.

When it comes to Web design, we might feel out of our element because we can't put our hands on a finished product and touch it. There's a tactile quality to print design that's missing from the Internet—there's no doubt about that. But as you read through these pages, you'll learn about a new way of seeing Web design that will help you see coding as a way of sculpting: how it has symmetry, balance, and form.

Think about when you spec paper for a project, how you have total control over the way your design turns out. You choose specific typefaces, solid-metallic inks, different paper stocks, varnishes, die-cuts, emboss, deboss, trimmed dimensions—everything comes together to create the final form.

One major difference between the medium you're used to and the Internet is that when you release a Web design project into the wild, you relinquish control over that final form. Your design will be rendered in oodles of different screen sizes; some viewers will have jacked up the color settings on their monitors; and certain fonts may not be available.

But it's not all doomy and gloomy. It's actually empowering to think of how your design can be flexible and work effectively in spite of these inconsistencies. The trick is a mental one for designers—learning to embrace the flexibility of the Web. As you start coding in the next few chapters, you will be introduced to concepts for flexible designs that don't even exist in print design.

And that's the fun stuff: things like variable widths, positioning images with percentages, font sizes that scale up or down gracefully, and more. Before you can learn to code, you will need to embrace the medium of the Internet.

THINGS WEB DESIGN CAN DO THAT PRINT DESIGN CAN'T

I wish I could show you some of these techniques in print, but I can't—that's sort of the point. Go to cssforprintdesigners.com/tactileweb to see a few examples of things you can do with Web design that you can't do with print design.

Three Steps to Thinking Like a Web Designer

When I started designing for the Web, I struggled to understand three things.

First and foremost, I struggled to accept that I, the designer, was not in control of everything any more. I scolded coders who told me my design was impractical. I came to terms with letting go after I started coding my own designs, which helped me gain an understanding of what goes in to a finished Web design and how it comes out.

What goes in is CSS and HTML—I can control this.

What comes out is the way the design looks on everyone's screen—I cannot control this.

By understanding these two things, I am able to see new opportunities to make my Web designs better for everyone. It will take time to move past thinking like a print designer, but with practice you can do it.

Step 1: Stop Being Such a Control Freak

Coder: "Is that 3200-pixel radial gradient necessary? It's going to make the page load really slow. And do you really want your body copy, all 5000 words of it, to be in Trajan?"

Me: "It's in the *design*, man. The client already signed off on it. Just figure it out."

Coder: "I hate my life. Do you care about IE6?"

Me: "What's IE6?"

Coder: "The blue *e* on the desktop."

Me: "Shyeah."

Coder: "I need a case of Mountain Dew. I'm going to be here for the next six nights. Again."

I tell you this for a good reason. While the end product of print design is a finished, precise, physical object, the Internet doesn't produce a finished thing; it's optimized to change form and adapt to its context. Since our job as designers is to strengthen ideas visually, we need to design for the Internet so information can change form gracefully (FIGURE 2.1).

FIGURE 2.1 Notice how on ethanmarcotte.com the same Web site looks different on different-size screens. The graphics stretch to fill the larger screen and shrink to fill the smaller screen. Additionally, Ethan has accounted for mobile browsers with his design. You can't do this with print design.

We need to stop being control freaks not because we can't control Web designs the way we're used to in page layout (though sometimes we really can't), but because the nature of the Internet means the design is going to change, no matter what we do. We need to accept this reality and design for flexibility.

This is the medium of the Internet. It's not just different screen sizes; it's different contexts and user empowerment. It's not just look and feel; it's the meaning of the words on the screen.

Step 2: What Goes In: Meaning Through HTML

If paper-and-ink is the medium of print design, the medium of the Internet is HTML and CSS. HTML gives meaning to the content, while CSS tells it what to look like.

Understanding how your designs will change from screen to screen is the first step to taking control over your design. We do this by writing HTML, before we ever start using CSS to tell it how to look.

HTML, while familiar sounding as a Web design language, is something print designers aren't used to thinking about. That's because print designers don't read the words their copywriters give to them. Okay, well, some of you do. But I'm here to tell you as a Web designer, whether you currently read the content your copywriter gives you or not, you need to *start* reading it. That's because you can't write HTML without reading your content.

So What Is This HTML Anyway?

Let's take a moment to understand what exactly HTML stands for: Hypertext Markup Language. Ouch, that sounds complicated. Do you really need to know what that means? Nope, not in my book you don't. Should you memorize it? Nah. Just know that sometimes HTML is referred to as markup, and sometimes coders will talk about "marking up" a page, which means "writing HTML."

Before you started this chapter, you may or may not have been familiar with HTML. A lot of print designers have at least heard of it and understand HTML as the coding language that you use to make things bold, or that's used for search engine optimization (SEO) with <h1> tags. Some of you might have even known that HTML and CSS need to hook together to work. That's a good start, but HTML is much more meaningful than that, as I hinted above.

We'll take a deeper dive into this later. For now, in short, HTML is how you tell the world what your content means. As an example, <h1> is a very important snippet of HTML that gets used on almost every Web site. It's an abbreviation for "Heading 1" and tells Google what your most important headline is.

Step 3: What Comes Out: Screen Sizes

For the purpose of this book, we're not going to discuss every possible con-figuration of screen sizes. Exploring all those combinations would be like trying to introduce you to every paper line by every paper manufacturer in the world. That is to say, it would be impossible and not very helpful. At some point, it becomes redundant (FIGURE 2.2).

FIGURE 2.2 There are tons of screen sizes and resolutions out there, everything from big computer screens to small mobile devices.

Instead, we'll focus on learning the easiest, most important 80 percent. Let's start with a normal Web site. That is to say, let's not worry about the expanding world of the mobile Web or your grandma's WebTV, or your iPad-optimized Web app. Let's focus on a plain ol' normal Web site.

We're starting with the basics because that's really all you need to know right now. And it's fundamental and simpler. Also, currently there's more traditional Web design work out there than other types of design work. And those other mobile devices are introducing new resolution technologies that make what you are about to learn seem like child's play. Baby steps.

How Big Should We Make Our Designs?

When we design for the Internet, we have to decide how big to make our designs. If we make them too big, users have to scroll left and right, which is annoying. If we make them too small, we're not taking advantage of the real estate that our users' larger screens afford us. So how do we decide?

By now, most of the modern world is on a computer with a resolution at or above 1024 pixels wide. We sit with our faces just a couple of feet away from them, so even with the larger screens out there, there's a lot of evidence that we don't need to keep designing bigger and bigger Web sites.

HORIZONTAL AND VERTICAL RESOLUTIONS

You're probably used to hearing screen sizes referred to with both horizontal and vertical dimensions, such as "1024 by 768." I'm intentionally avoiding this, and opting instead to refer only to the width, for two reasons.

First, it's simpler and potentially less confusing to refer just to the width, because screens with different proportions will have different vertical resolutions.

But more importantly, I want you to stop thinking about making Web pages that "fit" on a certain resolution. That's an old school remnant from the days of AOL where users were trained not to scroll because they had everything on the screen in a Web portal view. We're living in a time where our users are in the habit of scrolling down long pages. As long as there's an indication that there's something down below, they'll scroll.

Most people with big screens are taking advantage of the extra screen real estate by running multiple applications with multiple windows open. What this means is that a user who's browsing the Web on her 2560-pixel 27-inch iMac will likely have other windows open and scattered across her screen. For the most part, her browser window will be set to the size most Web sites are designed for, which is to say her browser will be around 1024 pixels wide (FIGURE 2.3).

Let's simplify this for you. Even for screens that are 1024 pixels wide, we wouldn't actually design our Web sites to be exactly 1024 pixels across because vertical scroll bars take up around 30 pixels of space. In addition, each user has idiosyncrasies that will impact the actual dimensions of her windows, such as whether or not she hides her dock or task bar by default, or whether she has additional toolbars installed on her browser.

FIGURE 2.3 I take advantage of my large monitor by multitasking, often listening to music while browsing and working at the same time. In the past, smaller screen sizes limited people to working in one application at a time, so screen size correlated to how big we should design our pages. Not so any more.

With all of these variables out there, my recommendation is to pick a size slightly under 1024. There's been a lot of fuss in the Web design world over the last few years about the 960 grid. Not every site should adhere to a 960 grid, but, as a general-purpose starting place for typical Web sites, a 960 grid is great because it gives you a lot of mathematical options for making columns. It's divisible by 2, 3, 4, 5, 6, 8, 10, 12, 15 and 16. With that math, the grid possibilities are almost endless.

Sometimes, you should design bigger layouts, or layouts that expand to fill a screen. This can be helpful for complicated Web applications and super sexy marketing sites. On the other hand, simple Web applications or marketing sites might not need to take up 960 pixels across. Use your best judgment when deciding which resolution is best for your design. There's no single answer for every situation.

Setting Up Your Web Design Files

I am always asked in my workshops what tools I use to design. I use Photoshop when it comes to comping out finished page layouts. But when it comes to planning your Web site before you start designing graphics, you need to know what tools are at your disposal.

The Toolkit for Web Designers

Believe it or not, there's a place in the Web design process for the apps you're accustomed to using day in and day out for page layout. You see, before you can start designing the finished graphics, you need to have a road map for the page layout. You might have heard this called storyboarding, wireframes, or a site flow.

I use InDesign (and even Illustrator) from time to time to quickly mock up a rough idea of what elements go on the page and where they go. These programs help me to work faster. As you know, InDesign is very good at flowing long body copy, and it has the added benefit of easily creating a multipage PDF for client reviews (FIGURE 2.4).

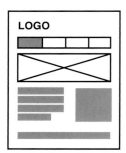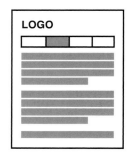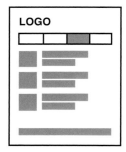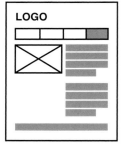

FIGURE 2.4 Wireframes can be created in Illustrator or InDesign to save time. They are useful in planning out your Web site before you start designing in a raster-based program like Photoshop.

Sometimes, though, InDesign wireframes have the unintended consequence of looking too finished. This can lead to confusion with clients, who think my clean, finished-looking grey wireframes mean I'm proposing a minimal, grey interface for their site. I have to admit, I can see why they'd be confused.

PHOTOSHOP VS. FIREWORKS

Both Photoshop and Fireworks are used by a lot of people for Web design. Some people feel very strongly about one over the other. I use Photoshop for mocking up Web pages, but you can use whichever one you prefer. I default to Photoshop in this book because more print designers are familiar with it. Either way, the principles in this chapter hold true for both applications.

When that's likely to happen, I'll use Balsamiq to create rough page layout ideas for client reviews (FIGURE 2.5). This handy application lets me present ideas to clients without running the risk of them interpreting my work as designed at all. It uses a pencil sketch graphic interface so that there's no doubt as to how preliminary the ideas are.

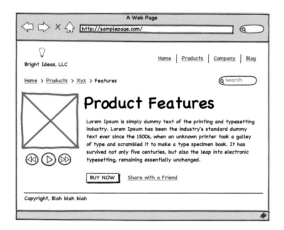

FIGURE 2.5
An application like Balsamiq can help keep your clients from confusing functionality with design aesthetics.

Once the site structure has been determined, that's when I'll open Photoshop to lay out the pages with the final graphics at the size they'll be in the finished Web design.

A New Workflow

You have the creative brief in hand, signed-off wireframes paper-clipped on your desk, a strong concept in mind, and an unlimited iStockPhoto account. It's go time.

You close down the print designer's trusty version of InDesign and fire up your Web design application of choice. As you move your mouse to the top left of your screen and click File, New Document, you consider the options before you. You are frozen with anxiety. A wrong step now can be a huge waste of time. Inches? Pixels? Points? Color Mode? Ten-twenty-who?

Let's take a break here to talk about the way you've been designing. As a print designer, you only open Photoshop to edit the color of an image or remove a stray nosehair from the CEO's headshot. From your days as a pre-presser (the best around, when you ran that department, we all know), your Photoshop workspace is optimized for a print workflow.

And it makes sense. It's literal. You likely have your Color Settings set to CMYK for four-color offset printing with real ink. Your units are something you understand—inches (or even picas, if you kick it old school). The size of your document has a direct correlation to the physical size of your end product. Five inches across by seven inches tall is five inches across by seven inches tall. Simple.

But with the Web, you need to change your workflow. Photoshop is mostly a raster graphics application, and Web graphics are, for the most part, raster as well, since they're output to a pixel-based monitor rather than a plate for a printing press. Also, Photoshop is great at saving graphics for the Web. The way you save your graphics when you export them matters— this can mean the difference between a crisp looking file that downloads at lightning speed or an artifacted JPEG that takes eight seconds to download on a corporate network.

So put away your loupe, your steel ruler, and your X-Acto knife. Let's push some pixels. You need to decide how big you want your Web site to be, what units of measurement to use, and what the color settings need to be. The problem is, as you well know, not everyone has a 27-inch iMac like you: Your site's viewers will have 15-inch Dells, 10-inch netbooks, monitors set to 1024 pixels or 1280, and so on. Will it fit on everyone's screen? Let's take a detour here to learn a little about how screens work so we can make an informed decision on how to proceed.

Understanding Resolution: From Billboards to Computer Screens

In the print design world, when we're not using solid colors, we have a dot pattern. We love going to press checks and staring at dot patterns through our trusty loupes. We grumble under our breath at pressmen when the registration's off and our crisp edges get fuzzy. When we hold a finished piece in our hands, assuming the registration is right, the dots are small and indistinguishable from one another—this makes the imagery crisp.

When we design for billboards, we have very large files because of the physical dimensions of the project. These files can become unwieldy, so we have figured out ways to make file sizes smaller. We know dots-per-inch can be much lower and still look crisp from the road since bigger dots are indistinguishable when viewed from a distance, so we have a lot lower setting for dots-per-inch when designing billboards. No sense in making a large file just so it looks crisp up close if no one will ever see it up close. If you were to fling a grappling hook over a billboard one night and climb up there to look at it from a couple of feet away (this is unsafe, illegal, and I don't recommend it), you would see the lower dots-per-inch and notice how the billboard doesn't look crisp up close like it does from down at street level.

With computer screens, we are working with the same basic laws. We want to make the files as small as possible for download speed, but make them high enough resolution so imagery looks crisp. For a typical Web site, you need to set up your files at 72 dots per inch (dpi). This is sometimes called pixels per inch (ppi).

Trust me, there's a lot of science behind this; it's all very complicated and makes my brain ooze out through my eye sockets just thinking about it. In short, it's the same in principle as the billboard scenario described above: We go with 72 dpi for Web design because it creates smaller files for down-loading and looks pretty good to the naked eye from a couple of feet away (the distance from your screen to your face).

Understanding Color: From PANTONE to RGB

As print designers, we're familiar with PANTONE's Matching System (PMS) for colors. Basically, we have this little book we all use that gives professional printers the ingredients to make colors exceptionally consistent. It's awesome.

Sadly, there's no universal color matching system for Web design. Backlit screens, for the most part, use three colors (red, blue, and green) to make up the images that display on them. But just like the light bulbs in your house might have different tones if you bought different brands at different times, computer screens from different manufacturers don't all have the exact same red, blue, and green. Some are brighter, some are warmer, and some are cooler.

Furthermore, even if screen manufacturers standardized their colors, users have different preferences and will change the settings of their screens to suit themselves. Some will turn up the brightness, some will make every-thing cooler, and some will prefer a warmer display.

COLORS THAT YOU REALLY SHOULD BE CAREFUL WITH

- Light yellows and tans are really difficult colors to work with. They may look great on your screen and green on someone else's.

- Because of different brightness settings, extremely light or dark colors are always hard to get right. A deep charcoal grey texture might look black on one screen and too light on another. Often, a subtle hairline rule might not be visible on some screens.

Since every manufacturer has slightly different colors and every user has slightly different color settings, your colors will look slightly different across everyone's computer screen. There's no way to control this. So, if your company has a purple PMS for its logo, you can match it pretty closely online, but it's always going to look slightly different on different people's screens.

Finally, Setting Up Your First Web Design File

Download the video clips for this book from **www.peachpit.com/ cssforprintdesigners** (Register at the site.)

Now that I've given you the background, let's cut to the chase. After setting your document preferences to use pixels instead of inches for your unit of measurement, here's all you need to know: 72 dpi, RGB (FIGURE 2.6).

FIGURE 2.6 Here are the settings for most of my Web design projects in Photoshop.

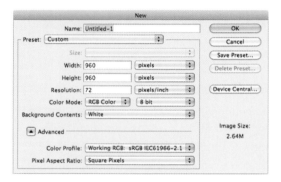

I could have just told you that in the beginning, but who's going to pay for a book with a two-word-long chapter?

3

Dump Drag and Drop

Learn How to Hook Things Together with Paths

WHEN I TEACH my workshops, I only have three hours to teach print designers how to code Web sites by hand. For this reason we spend a lot of time talking about the high-level stuff. This works out great for me because when the workshop's over, everyone is super excited about how much they learned in such a short time, and by how easy it was. The attendees give me credit for this. But the truth is, as soon as they get back to their desks and play with a Web site, they soon have questions about things I didn't cover in detail. Fortunately, the high-level approach gives them what they need to go forth and Google.

The workshops are designed this way intentionally. I'm more concerned with lowering barriers to entry than I am with covering everything in detail. In a lot of ways, this book is designed the same way—I don't expect you to know everything you need to know about coding Web sites by hand when you're done reading it.

In this book, though, I can take a little more time to explain a couple of things I have to breeze through in my workshops. One of these topics is how to write paths: I usually gloss over it because you can understand how to think about coding Web sites without understanding paths in depth. But the subject always bubbles up when you actually start to code a site. This chapter will give you the know-how to navigate a folder structure for a Web site and write efficient navigation links in HTML—in other words, it will teach you how to find your way around in a Web site.

Why You Shouldn't Rely on Software to Set Up Your Paths

Sure, there are tools that let you drag and drop Web pages and files into directories (which creates paths), but that's not hand-coding, is it? You bought this book to learn how to hand-code Web sites, and I intend to give you your money's worth.

Plus, when you're troubleshooting something that's broken, if you don't know how to do this you will be helpless. Trust me, you *will* be trouble-shooting broken things very soon, and you *will* feel helpless.

It's best to pay special attention to this chapter. It will give you the tools you need to fix 89.6 percent of the things that will break during your first two weeks of coding.

Web Sites Have Folders Like Your Computer

To understand paths, let's start with what you already know: organizing files and folders on your computer. When you're coding a Web site, you hook things together by typing their paths rather than by clicking into folders and files. You've probably heard this word *path* before.

A path looks like this on your Mac:

```
/Users/jdgraffam/Downloads/somefile.pdf
```

You start at the top level and go into folders by typing their name. You follow each folder name with a backslash. Then you go into another folder by typing its name. And on and on until you get the filename you want to open. That's really all there is to it.

GIVE IT A TRY

On a Mac: In Firefox, type `/Users/username/`, making sure to replace username with your username (**FIGURE 3.1**).

On a PC: In Internet Explorer, type `C:\Users\username`, making sure to replace username with your username.

Both of the examples above should pull up a listing of files and folders in your user folder. Notice how your browser will let you click around and navigate the folders and open some files. As you click around, pay special attention to the address bar where you typed in the path initially. Notice how the path changes based on where you are. All of this happens behind the scenes when you're browsing folders on your computer.

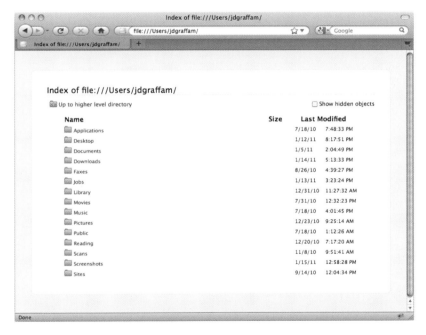

FIGURE 3.1 Typing a file path directly into Firefox lets you see how paths are formed by your computer behind the scenes.

Microsoft's Windows and Apple's Mac OS X are so easy to use because they give you a visual representation of your computer's file structure using folder icons that are nested hierarchically. Some of you are in the habit of creating new folders constantly to help organize your stuff; some of you prefer to dump everything into a single folder (**FIGURE 3.2**).

FIGURE 3.2 This is an example of a typical system folder.

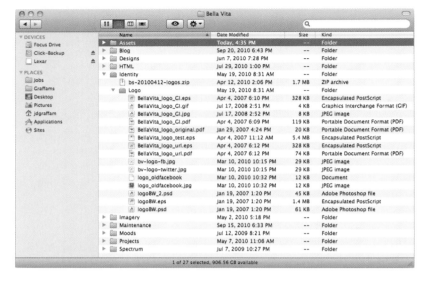

In either case, you're a working professional in the twenty-first century, so you know what folders are for and how to get around on your computer. You've probably even used a File Transfer Protocol (FTP) client at some point to upload large files to a file server.

WHAT'S A SERVER, EXACTLY?

A server is nothing more than a special computer that shares files or Web sites with the rest of the world. Your computer can run Web sites on it, but unless you know what you're doing, the stuff on your computer is only accessible by you.

How FTP Works (the Oversimplified Version)

In case you haven't used FTP before, or if you need a refresher, it's simple. Technically, FTP is just a method of moving files around the Internet—from a hard drive to a server (or vice versa) or from server to server.

Print designers often use FTP applications to transmit very large files that are too big to e-mail and when there's not enough time to burn the files to a DVD and mail it. Web designers use FTP to place files on a Web server so that they can go live on the Internet. Generally, when you deposit a file somewhere via FTP, it's referred to as *uploading*. When you retrieve a file via FTP, it's called *downloading*.

Popular FTP software for the Mac includes Transmit, Cyberduck, Fetch, and FileZilla. Popular FTP utilities for Windows include WS_FTP, SmartFTP, and FileZilla.

You'll typically connect to a Web server with an FTP address, username, and password. Once you have successfully logged in, you'll drag your files and folders from your computer (also called your *local drive*) to the Web server (also called the *remote drive*). Once they're on the Web server, your site is live.

You need to be careful as you work on your local drive editing your Web site that you use the most updated files from the remote drive.

Navigating Folders on the Internet

Basically, a Web site is a folder on a Web server with stuff inside it. It uses folders (also called *directories*) just as your computer does. The only difference is that when you're coding a Web page and you want to link or hook to another file, you can't click around to it—you need to know how to navigate to it by typing text paths, as you practiced in the previous section.

SOME THINGS YOU NEED TO HOOK TOGETHER

If you want your site's home page to link to the style definitions in your CSS file, you need to link them together by typing the path where your CSS file is saved. If you want to pull in your logo, you need to identify the path to it. If you want to link to another Web page, you need to point to it. Here's what that looks like:

CSS: src="css/base.css"
Images: src="images/logo.gif"
Link: href="login/"

The path is the text string between the double tick marks. Sometimes you'll describe the path using src= and other times you'll use href=. Don't worry about that right now, though; you'll learn all about that in a later chapter.

It's Like Packaging InDesign Projects

Let me explain it in a way that's always made sense to me with my print design background. Linking files on the Internet is similar to packaging InDesign files (FIGURE 3.3). InDesign creates folders for your fonts and images so that everything's all in one place for the next designer who's going to work on your project. When you import the package from someone else into your computer, you need to make sure everything gets relinked so that the paths are right. If the paths are wrong, you aren't able to use the fonts you want and the images aren't print-ready (FIGURE 3.4).

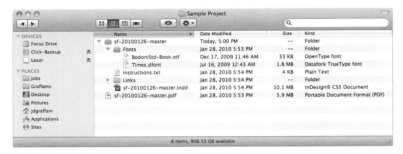

FIGURE 3.3 You are already familiar with the way InDesign packages files for delivery (as shown here). The Internet requires us to package files similarly, but you have to do it by hand.

FIGURE 3.4 InDesign helps you relink files without you having to know how to type the file path by hand.

InDesign is smarter than the Internet; so if you link something incorrectly you at least get a low-res preview and a warning that your fonts are missing (FIGURE 3.5) and a walk-through for fixing the problem (FIGURE 3.6). On the Internet, you don't get a low-res preview or any warnings. It just looks broken (FIGURE 3.7).

When it's time to start linking files together in your HTML page, you just need to type its path, rather than clicking to it, as you would do in InDesign. It's not as hard as it sounds, so there's no need to panic. There are two ways to go about this: You can use absolute paths or relative paths.

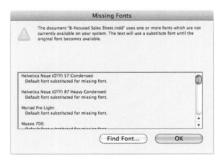

FIGURE 3.5 InDesign warns you when your fonts cannot be located.

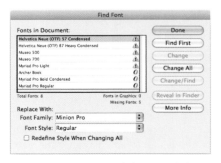

FIGURE 3.6 InDesign helps you relink your fonts without having to type their paths by hand.

FIGURE 3.7 On the Internet, when something is broken there aren't any warnings. It's just broken.

KEEPING YOUR FILES AND FOLDERS ORGANIZED

With InDesign you have the liberty to keep your files spread out all over your computer because it pulls all your files into a nice clean folder when you're ready to package them. When you're coding by hand, you need to manage this from the start of your project by saving everything in a single parent folder (FIGURE 3.8).

It's OK to have multiple folders: You just need a single parent folder where your site lives. It's also a good idea to keep stuff that isn't part of the finished Web site in another folder. This way the finished Web site files are separate from the working files.

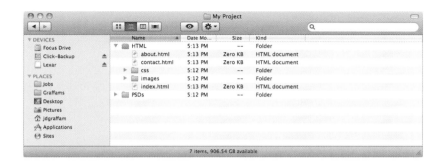

FIGURE 3.8
When you're packaging files for the Internet, keep your design files separate from your final assets.

Absolute Paths

Absolute paths are easier to understand for beginners because that's how we're used to seeing links on the Internet. If your Web site is located at cssforprintdesigners.com and you have a file in the main folder called mysecretfile.html, you would be able to navigate to that file using a Web browser by typing the following:

cssforprintdesigners.com/mysecretfile.html

The only thing you need to know is that files and folders are always followed with a backslash. If mysupersecretfile.html is located in a folder called supersecretfolder, you would navigate to it by going to

cssforprintdesigners.com/supersecretfolder/mysupersecretfile.html

When typing absolute paths in HTML, you need to type http:// at the beginning of the address, as follows:

http://cssforprintdesigners.com/supersecretfolder/mysupersecretfile.html

Relative Paths

Absolute paths are easy to understand because you're typing the entire path to the file from the very beginning, including the domain name. But this can be problematic if you want to move a site to a new domain. This happens a lot when your firm develops a site on its own server, like this:

myfirm.com/clients/ourclient/

When it comes time to move the site live to ourclient.com, you would need to find every instance of myfirm.com/clients/ourclient/ and change it to ourclient.com. While this is doable using a simple find and replace, it's easy to make a mistake; plus, there's a better way with relative paths.

Relative paths are just what they sound like. The file you are looking for is found not by an absolute path, but by its *relation* to where you're at currently.

Assume you have this folder structure (FIGURE 3.9):

- mydomain.com (folder)
  - images (folder)
    - logo.gif (file)
  - index.html (file)
  - pages (folder)
    - about.html (file)
    - contact.com (file)
  - private (folder)
    - index.html (file)

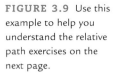

TIP Relative paths always assume you're starting inside the folder that contains the file you're editing.

FIGURE 3.9 Use this example to help you understand the relative path exercises on the next page.

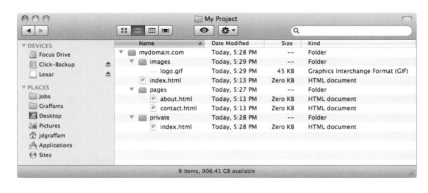

Moving Within the Same Folder

Let's say you're editing about.html in the pages folder. You want to link to contact.html in the same pages folder. All you'd need to type is contact.html since it's in the same folder. Simple.

Moving Into Deeper Folders

Let's try one that's a little more difficult. If you're editing index.html in the main folder (also called the root folder), and you want to link to about.html in the pages folder, you do it just as you did with the absolute paths, but you leave off the domain name. In fact you'd leave off anything above where you're currently at. Since you're at the root folder, all you have to leave off is the root folder. You'd just type pages/about.html.

Moving Into Higher Folders

Let's say you're editing contact.html and you want to link to index.html in the root folder. In other words, what we just did, but in reverse. Just as a backslash provides a shorthand way to go deeper into our folder structure, relative paths give us a shorthand way of going up one level. You type ../ to navigate up one folder. So what you'd type would be ../index.html to locate the index.html file that's one folder above where you're currently at.

If you need to go up two folders at once, you just type ./ instead of ../. You can also combine these to go up several folders at a time. ../../ is the same as ./ and ./.../ goes up four folders. Don't ask me why two dots means one folder and one dot means two folders—it just does.

Putting It Together

Now let's go crazy. Say you're editing about.html and you want to link to logo.gif in the images folder. Since we're going up a folder, then back deeper into another folder, we have to combine what we've learned up to this point. It helps to start by saying what we want to do in plain English first, so let's give that a try.

What we want to do is navigate up one folder, then we want to go deeper into the images folder so we can get to logo.gif. So we'd start by typing ../ to go up one folder, then we'd type the name of the folder we want to go in. So far we've gotten to ../images/. Now we just name the file and we're done: ../images/logo.gif. We went up one, we went into the proper folder, then we typed the name of the file.

Starting at Home

No matter where you're at, you can jump to the root folder by leading your path off with a backslash. For example, /images/logo.gif will link to the logo graphic no matter where you're at in the folder structure.

Leaving Off Index

The Internet has a special filename called index (or sometimes default) that you don't always need to include. So if you wanted to navigate to /login/index.html you could just put /login/ and leave off index.html.

Trailing Slashes

When you end with a folder, you should end with a trailing slash. When you end with a file, don't put the trailing slash—this will cause the Web server to treat your file like a folder, which you don't want.

These are correct:

/login/
/pages/about.html

This is wrong:

/pages/about.html/

This example would treat about.html like a folder name and cause the Web server to look for the index file in a folder named about.html, which doesn't exist.

This Chapter Will Fix 89.6 Percent of Your Problems—Read It Again

You'll remember I said 89.6 percent of your problems and frustrations will come from having the wrong paths. I know this because when I teach my workshops, I often have two assistants who help me out. Aside from helping everyone get on the wireless network at the university or hotel where we're having the workshop, which is way harder than it should be, their only job is to walk around during the part where everyone's coding their sites and help troubleshoot issues the attendees are having. After in-depth quantitative research (not really), I have confirmed that 89.6 percent of the time the problem is a wrong path.

Trust me, this chapter is worth a second or third read. I'd recommend bending the corner back on this chapter and coming back to it when you've finished the book.

You Have to Read the Words

This Is Not About Proofreading

THERE'S A REASON we designers are not allowed to send anything to the printer without having it proofread by a qualified individual. For designers, words and letters aren't much more than shapes interacting with one another. When we're in the zone, kerning our little hearts out, our minds aren't focused on meaning (FIGURE 4.1).

I'm not saying designers don't read—there's no way to art-direct a magazine layout or annual report without understanding the information being communicated. But let's be honest: Sometimes we skim. I mean, sure, headlines can be fun, but long copy is *boring*.

When we're setting type, we're thinking more about the aesthetic and readability of the words than we are about their grammatical significance.

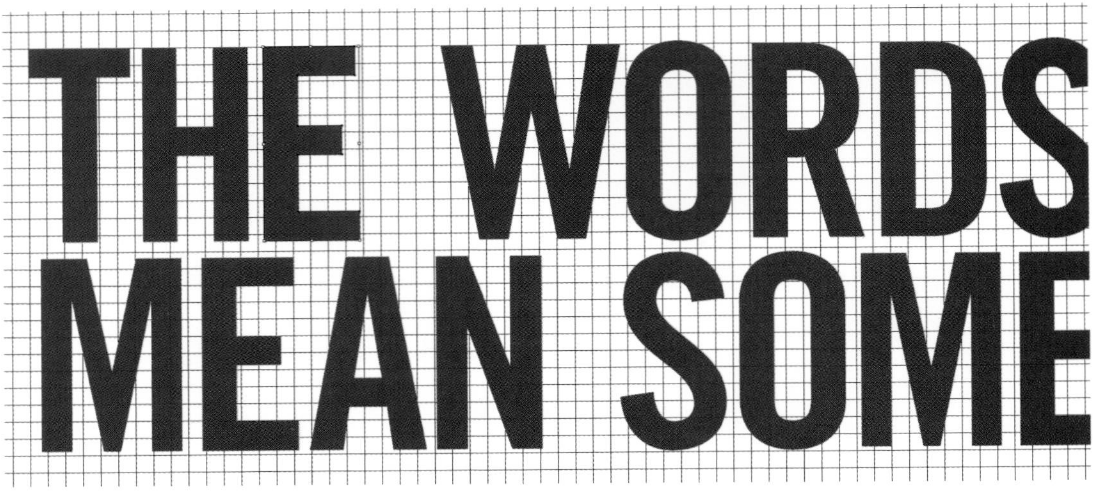

FIGURE 4.1 Kerning is fun. Reading is not.

It's the Whole Purpose of Coding

Before we start telling our Web pages what to look like with CSS, we code Web sites with HTML so the content we're designing can be shared in different ways. Additionally, CSS (the language that controls look and feel), is built on the structure of HTML—until you have a way of saying, "This is body copy," you can't write CSS to tell the body copy what to look like. HTML is that framework.

Let me explain this by demonstrating a problem you have probably faced from the print design world. If you need to lay out two brochures at different dimensions, you create a separate InDesign file and bring the content into each file separately. From then on, when your proofreader discovers a typo, you have to fix it in two places.

There's a concept in the Web design world where we separate content from the way it looks. You might hear of this as the separation of presentation from content. In short, it means that we maintain the content in one place and just reskin it with CSS to reuse it in different forms (FIGURE 4.2).

FIGURE 4.2 The content on Apple's homepage looks a certain way when you browse the Web site, but it looks different if you view it in an RSS reader.

So What Does HTML Do, Exactly?

HTML just tells us what sort of content we're looking at. To write HTML, you need to read the content from your copywriter so that you can identify what each chunk of content is. It's actually pretty simple, so don't freak out; here's a list of the main types of content you'll need to identify:

- **Paragraph:** A chunk of text; ideally it's a series of related sentences that create a unified thought.

  - HTML also lets you put breaks between chunks of content to mimic a soft return. Don't be fooled: Adding space below a chunk of text with a soft break is not the same as identifying it as a paragraph. HTML is not about what something *looks like*; it's about what it *is*.

- **Headline:** Summarizes the chunk of content that follows it.

  - Main headlines summarize the overall meaning of the following content, while the lesser headlines progressively summarize smaller, less global ideas.

  - HTML gives you six levels of headlines to pick from.

  - Typically, the more important the headline, the bigger it is. This is not always the case, though, which is why HTML exists. HTML helps you establish what the content *is* before you tell it what to *look like*. For example, you should work hard to ensure that <h3> tags are not above <h2> tags.

TIP When you cheat with HTML to get the look you want, you handcuff yourself because CSS isn't able to control the look and feel any more. One of the biggest advantages of using CSS to control look and feel is that look and feel is controlled in a single place.

- **List:** A series of related items.
  - HTML lets you work with a few different types of lists:
    - Unordered lists are what we typically call bulleted lists. But don't be fooled; not all unordered lists have bullet points. They might have arrows, or dashes, or squares. They might not even have these graphics at all. For example, navigation, which is a list of page links, does not. In case I haven't convinced you already, HTML isn't about what something *looks like*. It's about what it *is*.
    - Ordered lists are what we might call numbered lists. They can be 1., 2., 3... or i., ii., iii., etc. Use them when you're ordering items deliberately.
    - Definition lists have an item that's followed by some sort of definition or clarification. For example, a glossary of terms would use a definition list.
  - **Other stuff:** There are other little HTML chunks that you'll need to learn about that will let you emphasize, link, or group things together. But for now, paragraphs, headlines, and lists are the main ones I want you thinking about.

Using just the tags described above, your content can be displayed in an RSS feed or mobile-optimized Web site that has its own look and feel. It won't use the same typography or colors as your Web site, but it will be readable because it has HTML telling it which chunks of text are headings, paragraphs, and lists.

When your copywriter gives you a Word document, the document typically reads from top to bottom. It isn't pretty, but it's logical. Next time you get content from your copywriter, refer back to this section and try to identify each chunk of text the way HTML asks us to identify it. Just mark in the margins what each chunk of text is (FIGURE 4.3).

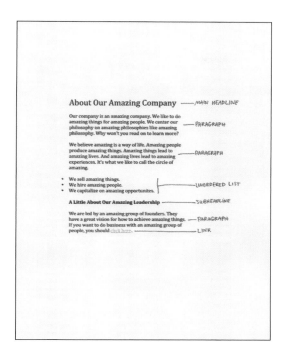

FIGURE 4.3 When you start writing HTML, it might help to put pen to paper and mark up the chunks of content.

If you ever get stuck trying to figure out how to identify a chunk of content, it wouldn't be a bad idea to check with your copywriter. Copywriters often use styles to format their documents, which you know can be mapped to InDesign. Similarly, this sort of structure could make your HTML writing easier.

Just like there's no *flow content* button that works for a 60-page technical manual you're designing with InDesign (boy, wouldn't that be nice!), there's no magic button that does this for coding Web sites—you have to use your brain.

5

Boxes Inside Boxes

Labeling Things Visually with HTML

IN MY WORKSHOPS I'm often asked how long it took me to learn CSS. Here's the story I tell.

I had been staring at code for several months before any of it made any sense to me. In fact, I bet a lot of you are in that spot right now. You can crack open Dreamweaver or WordPress and change the colors and widths of some things, but you're not sure exactly how it all works or what you might be breaking.

I've been there.

Learning CSS Happens Fast, Once You Know the Secret

It all came together for me during some training that Hilton Worldwide, my employer at the time, sent me to. You see, I sort of lied on my résumé and said I could do some things I couldn't. I say "sort of" for a reason. On my résumé I said I could code Web pages. I mean, I thought I could because I had a copy of Dreamweaver and could click Insert > Table. I could even update the year of the copyright in the footer once I found the right place. I knew how to upload files via FTP. Man, I was set.

Since I didn't realize I was lying at the time, I was only "sort of" lying.

At the time I had one of those rare bosses who knew what he was doing. He knew how to do my job as well as his own. He was reviewing my work one day just a few weeks after I started and clicked View > Source in a browser to look at my code.

Uh-oh, busted.

 "Go to training," he said, "Hilton will pay." So I went.

I found a two-day CSS for Beginners course in Atlanta, Georgia. This meant I got to get on a plane for work. My family was very impressed.

I, on the other hand, was nervous about losing my job. I didn't think the training would do me any good because the books I read on CSS made me feel like I was being dropped into the middle of a race that was already underway, like I was missing some foundational knowledge—where to begin.

So I landed in Atlanta, rented a car and drove out to a shaded business park where the training was happening. There was nothing especially remarkable about the building, the classroom, or the teacher. But after several hours of asking dumb questions, two basic things finally clicked for me and my entire career opened up:

1.   To write CSS, you have to know how to write HTML.

2.   HTML is made up of tags.

Let me repeat those two things again, because this is the foundational knowledge you need to write CSS: *You have to know how to write HTML first, and HTML is made up of tags.*

On the second day of class, I left for lunch and didn't bother coming back for the rest of the training—I had what I needed. Within two weeks, I was coding sites by hand on my own.

And you can learn it that quickly, too.

I had to trap myself in a room and ask a lot of dumb questions to get what I needed. Hopefully, you and your employer can avoid that expense and waste of time—the trick to writing CSS is knowing how to write HTML.

Once you know HTML, CSS doesn't take any time at all to learn. Yep, that's the secret to learning CSS—learning a completely different language.

HTML Is Made Up of Tags

Just as a tag on your luggage identifies whom the contents belong to, a tag in HTML identifies the stuff it contains. It must open, and it must close. It opens with a less-than and greater-than sign. It closes the same way, but with a slash.

HTML has three main parts:

1. An opening tag with an abbreviation inside it

2. The content that the abbreviation describes

3. A closing tag, with the same abbreviation inside it

I explain coding to print designers with varying levels of familiarity all the time. The one method I have used over and over with success is to pull out a stack of sticky notes and write HTML in a thick marker (FIGURE 5.1). Something about seeing HTML outside a computer, separated from the high-tech codeyness, makes the code more human and less intimidating.

 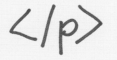

FIGURE 5.1
These sticky notes show how writing HTML is nothing more than surrounding chunks of content with an opening tag and a closing tag.

A Dozen Tags You Need to Know

There are about a hundred tags in all.

OK, stop hyperventilating. There's good news too.

The good news is that for the most part they're easy to remember because they're abbreviations of something that resembles plain English. The even better news is that you only need to know these 13 tags to get by.

These tags get me through 90 percent of my work day-to-day. If you know them, you will have a better understanding of what HTML is supposed to do.

- `<p>`

  We covered this already.

- `<header>`

  It's just what it sounds like. This tag surrounds the header for a section or an entire page. Most Web designers use this to surround their logo and primary navigation, but it can also surround the *header* of a smaller section of the page.

- `<footer>`

  Similar to header, this tag surrounds the footer of a section or an entire page.

- <h1>, <h2>, <h3>, <h4>, <h5>, <h6>

  Headings, or headlines, are usually short chunks of text that summarize what follows them. <h1> is the most important headline, and <h6> is the least important. You use your best judgment to identify heading levels, but ideally each page will have at least one <h1>.

- <ul> and <li>

  Some tags come in pairs (more on this below). An unordered list, or <ul>, is always paired with list items, or <li> tags. You would sometimes call this a bulleted list, though bullet points are not necessary.

- <ol> and <li>

  This is another paired set of tags. An ordered list, or <ol>, is always paired with list items, or <li> tags. You would call this a numbered list.

- <div>

  <div> is short for division. It doesn't imply any grammatical context like a paragraph or a headline; it's just a way to group large chunks of related things. It's usually used, in fact, to group paragraphs and headlines. What it surrounds is limited only by your imagination.

- <a>

  <a> stands for anchor. *Anchor* is HTML's way of saying *link*, so an <a> tag is just a link.

- <strong>

  The <strong> tag is what we use to surround short bits of text we think deserve a little more attention. Often, this is how we'd go about making something bold.

- <em>

  The <em> tag is what we use to surround short bits of text that we think deserve emphasis. Often, this is how we'd go about making something italic.

- <span>

  Like its big brother the <div> tag, the <span> tag is for grouping things. It's just used to separate out smaller groups, mostly just little bits of text.

- <img>

  <img> is short for image. This is how you bring in an image with HTML.

New HTML vs. Old HTML

HTML is undergoing some big changes right now. No need to worry, though, for you it's not that big of a deal. Basically, some new tags have been added (such as <header> and <footer>), which didn't exist before. Since you didn't know the previous tags, they're *all* new to you.

Here's the thing: HTML5 is being developed to replace HTML4—you should be learning HTML5, not HTML4. Simple as that.

It's just like how Adobe CS5 replaced CS4: It's just a newer version. As with Adobe's Creative Suite, HTML5 has some backward compatibility, but it's a little limited. But unlike Adobe's Creative Suite, the new HTML is an open standard that doesn't directly make money for anyone, so there's less incentive to update it than with a for-profit product. In fact, the new standard for HTML5 isn't finished, and it won't be for a long time.

Now don't go asking me why you should be learning something that's not finished. I want you learning the HTML of the future, not of the past. In my opinion there are no roadblocks to prevent you from using HTML5 for all your projects going forward.

Dealing with Older Browsers

As I mentioned above, HTML5 has a handful of tags that didn't exist before, including <header> and <footer>. I mention this because older browsers like IE and Firefox 2 don't acknowledge these newer HTML tags, which causes them to break your layout.

But don't worry, just as you can save back to an older version of InDesign, you can put some code in place on your Web pages that makes the older browsers play nice. These fixes rely on *JavaScript* to work.

You Mean I Need to Learn JavaScript?

God, no. I barely even know JavaScript. Since JavaScript is a little advanced for this book, I'm going to avoid talking about it much. All you need to know is there's a snippet of JavaScript that you can add to a Web site that helps older browsers understand the new tags from HTML5.

But right now, honestly, you don't need to worry about it. When it comes up, you can just have one of your coder friends help you out or Google for the snippet of code. That's what I do.

Tag Groups (Also Known as Lists)

You might have noticed I slipped in a couple of different looking tags: `<ul>` and `<li>` and `<ol>` and `<li>`. Those were for lists. Some tags, like lists, require you to use a couple of tags in combination for them to work.

This means you have to write some HTML that says, "I'm about to write a list." Then you have to write some more HTML inside that tag that says, "This is an individual list item." You can write all the list items you want, then you have to close the tag that started the list.

Unordered Lists (or Bullet Lists)

Okay, that's a lot to take in, so let's start with an unordered list. You'll remember an unordered list is made using the `<ul>` tag mentioned earlier. You'd write:

```
<ul></ul>
```

But that doesn't really make sense because it's an unordered list without any items, also known as *list items,* in it. There's a tag for that, called `<li>`, but it has to go inside of the unordered list tag, which means it has to open after the opening `<ul>` tag and close before the closing `</ul>` tag. See for yourself:

```
<ul>
  <li></li>
</ul>
```

Notice how we have moved the closing `</ul>` tag down and added the `<li></li>` on a single line, indented, between the opening `<ul>` and closing `</ul>` tags.

While formatting this way is completely optional, keep in mind that being able to easily match opening and closing tags visually by keeping consistent formatting will be very helpful as your HTML gets more complicated.

So we still only have one list item. Let's add a few more.

```
<ul>
  <li></li>
  <li></li>
  <li></li>
</ul>
```

Notice how each opening `<li>` tag closes with a closing `</li>` tag before we open a new list item.

Now, we still don't have a real list, all we have is some HTML tags waiting for content. Let's put something in there. Here's an example of what a print designer's grocery list might look like:

```
<ul>
  <li>Whole wheat bread</li>
  <li>Locally-brewed beer</li>
  <li>Organic cigarettes</li>
</ul>
```

Let's review. The outer tag, <ul>, tells us that we're about to start making an unordered list. The inner tag, <li>, defines each item for that list. So what you'd get would look something like this:

- Whole wheat bread
- Locally-brewed beer
- Organic cigarettes

Breakfast of champions.

You can change the way your bullet points look later (or get rid of them entirely) with CSS.

Ordered Lists (or Numbered Lists)

As you'll remember, there's another option when creating a list, called an *ordered* list. Let's look at what a list of your favorite bands, in order of preference, might look like:

```
<ol>
  <li>Mogwai</li>
  <li>Mouse Rat</li>
  <li>Lucero</li>
</ol>
```

This would render like so:

1. Mogwai
2. Mouse Rat
3. Lucero

With CSS, you can change this to render as:

i.   Mogwai
ii. Mouse Rat
iii. Lucero

We could go on all day about that musical awesomeness, but we're just here to learn how to make lists—move along.

Definition Lists (or Glossary Listings)

There's one final kind of list. So far we've covered bullet lists and numbered lists (unordered and ordered lists, respectively). The other kind of list, called a *definition list*, is less common but very useful.

First, let's take a look at what a definition list is, precisely. A definition list is made up of three tags:

1. `<dl>`, which defines that we're about to write a *definition list.*

2. `<dt>`, which defines the content it surrounds as a *definition title.*

3. `<dd>`, which defines the content it surrounds as a *definition description.* This tag follows the dt tag, but there can be more than one—think of it as similar to a paragraph. Once you see it in action, this will be more clear.

Definition lists can be used for a couple of things. Most often you'll see them used to mark up a glossary, but sometimes I have seen them used for Frequently Asked Questions. While we know we can change the appearance of anything with CSS, a typical definition list created by a print designer might look something like this:

Photoemulsion

A special liquid mixture that you put on screens. When it dries and you expose it to light it hardens. It's used to block the flow of ink through the screen. It's magic.

Image Area

If you block off part of the emulsion when exposing it to light, so that light doesn't get to all the photoemulsion, you can wash that area out since it doesn't harden.

This is the area where ink can pass through the screen to create your image.

Positive

A clear sheet with opaque black printed or drawn on it. This black area is what blocks the light from getting to the photoemulsion, keeping that area from hardening when exposed to light.

Here's how you would mark this up without the content inside.

```
<dl>
   <dt></dt>
   <dd></dd>

   <dt></dt>
   <dd></dd>
   <dd></dd>

   <dt></dt>
   <dd></dd>
</dl>
```

If you looked at that HTML closely (you did look at it closely, right? No? Go look again…), you noticed how the second grouping has one dt tag, but two dd tags. That's because the "Image Area" item has two blocks of text describing it. This is what I meant when I said it was *like* a paragraph.

Let's see how this would look with the content inside of it:

```
<dl>
   <dt>Photoemulsion</dt>
   <dd>
     A special liquid mixture that you put on screens. When it dries and
     you expose it to light it hardens. It's used to block the flow of
     ink through the screen. It's magic.
   </dd>
   <dt>Image Area</dt>
   <dd>
     If you block off part of the emulsion when exposing it to light, so
     that light doesn't get to all of the photoemulsion, you can wash
     that area out since it doesn't harden.
   </dd>
   <dd>
     This is the area where ink can pass through the screen to create your
     image.
   </dd>
   <dt>Positive</dt>
   <dd>
     A clear sheet with opaque black printed or drawn on it. This black
     area is what blocks the light from getting to the photoemulsion,
     keeping that area from hardening when exposed to light.
   </dd>
</dl>
```

That doesn't look as scary as it did before you started reading this book, now does it? By now you should be able to read through the code on the preceding page and pick apart its tags and see how they're in the right order. The less-than and greater-than symbols aren't nearly as confusing, now that you know what they do and how they work.

And the best part is: Most of it's *English*—it's really not that much to remember.

Sometimes, when code starts to look like too much for me, I'll highlight the code parts, to help simplify things. The preceding code block begins to look much less complicated when you focus on only the simple tags.

Here's what that might look like:

```
<dl>
  <dt>Photoemulsion</dt>
  <dd>
    A special liquid mixture that you put on screens. When it dries and
    you expose it to light it hardens. It's used to block the flow of
    ink through the screen. It's magic.
  </dd>
  <dt>Image Area</dt>
  <dd>
    If you block off part of the emulsion when exposing it to light, so
    that light doesn't get to all of the photoemulsion, you can wash
    that area out since it doesn't harden.
  </dd>
  <dd>
    This is the area where ink can pass through the screen to create your
    image.
  </dd>
  <dt>Positive</dt>
  <dd>
    A clear sheet with opaque black printed or drawn on it. This black
    area is what blocks the light from getting to the photoemulsion,
    keeping that area from hardening when exposed to light.
  </dd>
</dl>
```

Whenever you start reading HTML, the most important thing to watch for is the opening and closing of tags. Try to ignore everything else; read slowly; don't skim. Over time, you'll be able to skim well-formatted HTML and quickly spot errors. But right now, slow down. I want you to focus on reading HTML deliberately and finding each closing tag for each opening tag.

Nesting Tags

Since you've just been introduced to tag groups (or lists), now's a good time to zoom out and see what HTML looks like from 30,000 feet.

You see, a Web site is made up of lots and lots of HTML tags. Some of the tags are for defining each individual piece of content, like list items, and some HTML is there for defining much larger sections of content.

To make it all work, you're going to have to start *nesting* your HTML.

Nesting Tags Is Like Drawing Boxes Inside of Boxes

You just did this with lists. HTML tags nest inside of each other, much like the fancy nesting tables you might pick out from a CB2 catalogue. Print designers often understand this better when they look at a graphic that shows what nesting HTML looks like (FIGURE 5.2).

FIGURE 5.2 A diagram like this helps me to visualize nested HTML as boxes drawn inside of boxes.

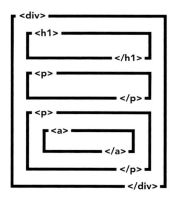

In code, it would look like this:

```
<div>
  <h1>My Very Own Headline</h1>
  <p>With a paragraph following it.</p>
  <p>
    <a href="http://mysite.com">Learn more</a>
  </p>
</div>
```

That's what nesting looks like when it's all clean and tidy. I'll do this exercise on the whiteboard when I'm trying to solve larger problems. Take a look at the same thing, using a little shorthand on a whiteboard (FIGURE 5.3).

FIGURE 5.3 When I am figuring out complicated HTML, I'll often mark it up visually on a whiteboard.

Breaking the Internet

When you make a mistake writing your HTML, it's often because you didn't open or close your tags the right way—which leads to a broken Internet, the whole thing, and it's all your fault.

Not really. But it will break your Web site almost every time. When you're nesting tags, they must close in the reverse order that they were opened (**FIGURE 5.4**).

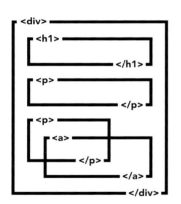

FIGURE 5.4 You have to make sure you open and close your tags in the right order. They can't overlap like the a and p tags at the bottom of this diagram.

Everything looks good until you get to the place where the <p> tag and the <a> tag cross each other. In code, that might look like this:

```
<div>
  <h1>My Very Own Headline</h1>
  <p>With a paragraph following it.</p>
  <p>
    <a ="http://mysite.com">Learn more</p>
  </a>
</div>
```

Did you catch that? In this example, the <p> tag closes before the <a> tag, which is wrong because the <a> tag opened inside the <p> tag. Since it opened inside the <p> tag, it should close inside the <p> tag.

I don't think any of us wants Al Gore knocking on our door demanding we fix his Internet. So take some time with this, be sure to open and close your tags in the right order.

Adding Attributes to Tags

The word *attribute* is kind of a big word, but I bet most of you know what it means without having to look it up. But just in case, and to keep you from having to haul out your dictionary, here's my definition: An *attribute* is a characteristic of something or someone.

If I asked you to describe the attributes of this fellow (FIGURE 5.5), you might say his hair is red and that he has cute cheeks. An attribute has to identify something and then describe it. With this image, I've chosen to identify two things about the boy and describe them.

In HTML, we use attributes to give more meaning or definition to tags.

FIGURE 5.5 This little boy has red hair and cute cheek attributes.

iStockPhoto.com

Attribute Syntax (Yes, a Few More Funny Characters to Memorize)

Attributes have a syntax that might look intimidating until you break it down. After you have cracked the code, they're just like HTML tags—that is, they're mostly English with a couple of funny characters to memorize. No big deal. As an example, let's take a look at what a fake attribute for this boy might look like:

```
hair="red"
cheeks="cute"
```

First, we identify what we're talking about: his hair and his cheeks. Then, we say it equals something, which we put in double tick marks.

But that's not the whole story. We have to put this somewhere, so you might be asking, "Where does this go?" An attribute in HTML goes *inside* the opening tag. Let's continue to use a fake HTML tag to describe this:

```
<boy hair="red" cheeks="cute">This boy has red hair and cute cheeks.</boy>
```

A few things to take note of:

- The attribute goes inside the opening tag. Nothing ever goes inside a closing tag.

- There is a single space before the attribute begins.

- There are no spaces once the attribute begins. There are a couple of exceptions to this rule, but nothing we need to worry about right now.

- We're using double tick marks, not curly quotes. If you're typing them directly into your text editor of choice (like Dreamweaver, Text Wrangler, or Coda, for example), you'll be fine because those applications won't automatically turn your tick marks into curly quotes. But if you copy and paste from Word, you might run into issues with curly quotes showing up.

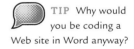 **TIP** Why would you be coding a Web site in Word anyway?

Five Attributes You Need to Know

Just like the 13 tags that get used more than others, there are five attributes you absolutely must know by heart when writing HTML. There are more, but these are the most important ones I want you to know about—they'll get you through 90 percent of your coding.

- `href`

   This attribute is for making links and goes with the `<a>` tag. When we start hooking CSS to HTML, we'll see how this attribute is used on the `<link>` tag, too. The string that goes inside this tag is either an absolute or relative path. (We discussed absolute and relative paths in Chapter 3.)

- class

  This attribute is for CSS hooks, and you can have many per page that match.

- id

  This attribute is for CSS hooks, and you can have only one per page. It's also used for jump links, where you click a link and it jumps the browser to a certain part of the page.

- src

  Every <img> tag requires this. It's for bringing an image into HTML.

- alt

  Every <img> tag requires this. It's for describing the image with words in case the image doesn't load. It's for Google, blind or low-vision users who listen to Web pages being read to them, and for really slow connections or images that don't load for some reason.

You can always go to the almighty Google to learn about the rest.

Attributes in Action

```
<a href="http://simplefocus.com/">This is a link to my company website</a>
<div id="something">Something goes in here</div>
<span class="something-else">Something else goes in here</span>
<img src="img/my-image.jpg" alt="Description of the image" />
```

The cool thing about attributes is that, for the most part, what goes inside of the double quotes isn't code. It's not something you need to memorize. You can make up your own class and id attributes. You can have class="bibbledibob" if you want, it doesn't matter.

Don't Go Crazy with Attributes

You do need to keep in mind that your class attributes should make sense to other people, though, because one day someone may work on your site after you. Or, even more likely, you'll come after yourself and wonder, "What was I thinking? That class attribute is just silly!"

As a responsible Web designer, I have to tell you to use good naming practices when you come up with id and class attributes. In the industry, this is called writing *semantic* HTML. *Semantic* is another big ugly word. But you might know what it means because print designers love to get into semantic arguments with each other on things like God and the kerning of Archer.

The word *semantic* in the Web design world has a similar definition. It means, ironically, *meaning*. Your class and id attributes shouldn't describe what something *looks like*; rather, they should describe what something *is*— remember the luggage tag analogy.

TABLE 5.1 Meaningful class Attributes (Also Applies to ids)

BAD	GOOD
class="yellow-background"	class="highlight"
class="left"	class="sidebar"
class="italic-headline"	class="embellished"
class="rounded-corner-effect"	class="wrap"
class="bigger-text"	class="callout"

Self-Closing Tags

So far you have learned about tags that open and close such as <header>, <p>, and <div>. What if I told you there were a few tags that can close themselves? Would that blow your mind?

Some tags don't need to wrap anything. Some tags are the information themselves, like the <img> tag.

If you were paying attention, you'd have noticed I slipped one of those into the section on attributes.

<img src="img/my-image.jpg" alt="Description of the image" />

Notice how this <img> tag doesn't have a separate closing tag. Instead, the opening tag is self-closing because there is a slash right before the closing angle bracket (or greater-than sign). This is called a self-closing tag. There are actually two correct ways to do this with HTML5:

1. <img src="img/my-image.jpg" alt="Description of the image" />

  or

2. <img src="img/my-image.jpg" alt="Description of the image">

Technically speaking, neither way is more correct since HTML5 supports both methods of self-closing a tag. I have a personal preference, but I do encourage you to consider both and make your own decision.

I prefer to use the trailing slash method (number 1 above) because it makes it easier for me to scan for tags that have been properly closed. I've trained myself to watch for an opening tag and search for its closing partner.

On the other hand, there's a good reason to go with the non-slash method (number 2): It has fewer characters to type.

It's up to you. Just pick one and stick with it.

Formatting Code Is Like Setting Type

A great question that always comes up in my workshops is about formatting.

- How do I know when to press Return and go to the next line?
- How do I know where it's safe to put spaces and where it's not safe to put spaces?
- How do I know when, or how far, to indent? Do I use tabs or spaces?

These are great questions. And while there is technically a correct answer from the powers that be about every bit of formatting, it comes in the form of recommendations. For you, here's what I want you to know about formatting.

However You Do It, Be Consistent

Although you are writing code for computers to understand, you have to remember it's for human consumption too. Establishing your own little nuances with formatting your HTML is fine. You're a designer, so think of this as an exercise in setting type for readability using only indents and a monospace typeface (FIGURE 5.6).

- If you prefer to indent with spaces instead of tabs, that's fine, just be consistent. Having too many spaces typically won't cause things to break, so don't sweat it.
- If you use hyphens when creating multiword class attributes, stick with hyphens. Don't randomly switch to underscores.
- Err on the side of human readability. If you can fit a couple of tags on one line because the content's short, do it. If you are doing some very heavy nesting, be careful to make sure your closing tags line up with your opening tags, so it's easier to see which tag is closing.

```
<header>
    <div class="utility-links">
        <ul>
            <li class="login">
                <a href="/login/">Login</a>
            </li>
            <li class="help">
                <a href="/help/">Help</a>
            </li>
        </ul>
    </div>
    <div class="wrap">
        <div class="logo">
            <img src="img/logo.gif" alt="Simple Focus Logo" />
        </div>
        <nav>
            <ul>
                <li class="home">
                    <a href="http://simplefocus.com/">Home</a>
                </li>
                <li class="about">
                    <a href="/about/">About</a>
                </li>
                <li class="services">
                    <a href="/services/">Services</a>
                </li>
                <li class="portfolio">
                    <a href="/portfolio/">Portfolio</a>
                </li>
                <li class="contact">
                    <a href="/contact/">Contact</a>
                </li>
            </ul>
        </nav>
    </div>
</header>
```

FIGURE 5.6 HTML is easier to read if you indent in a logical and consistent manner.

Using Comments to Stay Organized

Sometimes a coder needs to remind herself what she was thinking or communicate with another coder who will follow her work later. Rather than writing these notes somewhere else, HTML has a way for coders to write notes that are not rendered by the browser. These are called *comments*.

```
<!-- Comment goes here -->
```

The opening of the comment is indicated by <!--, which is where the browser stops paying attention. Whatever goes in there will not show up on your Web site. When you're done with your comment, just type --> to let the browser know to start paying attention again.

There are plenty of good reasons to use comments.

To indicate where a tag is closing. If you have a bunch of <div> tags nested with unique id or class attributes, you can remind yourself which one you're closing.

```
<div class="wrap">
  <div class="intro">
    <div class="summary">
      <p>
        Comments are helpful to developers because they facilitate clear
        ➡ communication.
      </p>
    </div><!-- close summary -->
    <div class="extended">
      <p>
        Some developers use comments to describe a complex area of the
        ➡ code, while other developers use them to help themselves
        ➡ remember what they were thinking when they came up with
        ➡ something. And finally, some developers use them to crack
        ➡ mom jokes about their colleagues (which is not appropriate and
        ➡ can be embarrassing if it makes it into a production site).
      </p>
    </div><!-- close extended -->
  </div><!-- close intro -->
</div><!-- close wrap -->
```

To communicate with another developer. Sometimes more than one person is working on the code, and they will need to communicate with each other.

```
<!-- Tom, I was thinking while we wait on content from the client,
➥ we could use CSS to put a drop shadow and round these corners around
➥ the content. What do you think? -->
<div class="content">
  <p>Waiting on content from the client.</p>
</div>
```

To remind yourself what you were thinking. Sometimes you come up with a great way to do something and you want to remind yourself how it works so you don't break it later.

```
<!-- Added an extra div with post class below so that I can have a
➥ divider between each blog post. Removing this breaks vertical
➥ spacing. -->
<div class="post">
<h2>Hello world!</h2>
  <p>
    Welcome to Wordpress. This is your first post. Edit or delete it,
    ➥ then start blogging!
  </p>
  <p>
    <a href="/hello-world">Read more</a>
  </p>
</div>
```

A comment can be whatever you want it to be. You just type a few characters to tell the browser to start ignoring what you're about to type, then you type a few characters to tell the browser you're done with the comment.

Block and Inline Tags

Of all the hundred or so tags out there, they all fall into one of two categories: They are either block tags or inline tags.

As simply as I can put it, block tags are for surrounding larger chunks of text, and inline tags are for surrounding smaller chunks of text. I like to think of block tags as energetic and inline tags as lethargic.

Block tags are energetic because they run as far as they can across the page from left to right. Inline tags are lethargic because they only go as far as they have to, then they quit.

In other words, a block tag's job is to take up as much horizontal space as it can within its parent container (it stretches as far as it can until it hits a dead end). An inline tag's job is to take up as little horizontal space as possible (FIGURE 5.7).

FIGURE 5.7 Block tags go as far as they can; inline tags only go as far as they have to.

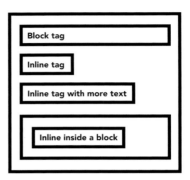

Of the tags I have shown you already, these are block-level tags:

- ‹p›
- ‹header›
- ‹footer›
- ‹h1›, ‹h2›, ‹h3›, ‹h4›, ‹h5›, ‹h6›
- ‹ul› and ‹li›
- ‹ol› and ‹li›
- ‹div›

And these are the inline-level tags:

- ‹a›
- ‹strong›
- ‹em›
- ‹span›
- ‹img›

Headlines and paragraphs, for example, should generally run the width of their parent container. On the other hand, an anchor (link) or ‹em› tag should not run the width of its parent container because those tags are typically found inside a larger string of text.

If you think about it, this would wreak havoc on a layout (FIGURE 5.8). An anchor tag that behaved like a block tag in the middle of a sentence would cause the line of text to break to a new line and the anchor would take up an entire line on its own. Then, whatever followed the anchor would start on the line after the anchor. In effect, it would create a hard break with the link on a line all by itself.

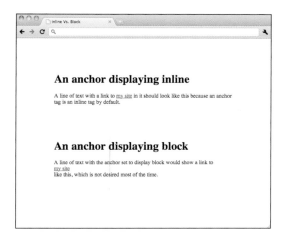

FIGURE 5.8 Block tags are meant to surround bigger chunks of text; inline tags are meant to surround smaller pieces of text.

The Order of Inline and Block Tags

You remember the concept of nesting, right? The way it works is that something smaller goes inside something bigger. If we think of block tags as bigger than inline tags, then it doesn't make sense for us to put block tags inside inline tags, does it (FIGURE 5.9)?

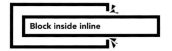

FIGURE 5.9 You cannot put a block tag inside an inline tag; it will break things!

There's one simple rule you need to know: Inline tags cannot surround block tags.

Changing the Appearance of Inline and Block Tags

You can change the appearance of block tags to behave like inline tags, or to make inline tags behave like block tags.

Using CSS, you can tell a block tag to display: inline; and it would behave like an inline tag. Or, you could tell an inline tag to display: block; and it would behave like a block tag. This can be a very useful trick, for example, if you want to make a link that has a defined width or is bigger and easier to click, like in your navigation.

But, you still have to follow the rule that states native block tags cannot go inside inline tags. Sorry, rules are rules—plus, your site needs to work properly for users before CSS comes in and makes everything pretty.

More on CSS ahead. Stay calm. We'll get there.

One last thing you should know about HTML: Since its purpose is nothing more than structuring content, when you finish writing HTML, it's pretty easy to tell if you did it right.

HTML Looks Like a Word Doc

Download the video clips for this book from **www.peachpit.com/ cssforprintdesigners** (Register at the site.)

When you're done writing HTML with a text editor, you can save the file on your computer somewhere and open it with your browser (Firefox, Chrome, Safari, or Internet Explorer) by choosing File > Open and then browsing to the file.

When you pull up your HTML file, if everything's in order, your HTML document will pretty much resemble your copy writer's Word doc (FIGURE 5.10).

FIGURE 5.10
When you're done writing HTML, it should look pretty much like the Word doc you started with.

Now that we've gotten that out of the way, we have something that looks exactly like what we started with.

No, the irony is not lost on me. Unfortunately, learning this stuff is the unavoidable prerequisite to writing CSS.

Let's move on.

6

Sculpting with CSS

Making Something That Looks Like a Real Web Page

I THINK OF writing CSS as being a lot like creating a sculpture because both CSS and sculptures are deliberate, planned processes of whittling a basic structure into a more beautiful form.

The sculptor starts with a big square block of stone, or wood, or some other material. When we write CSS, we start with an HTML structure that reads top to bottom like a basic Word document.

The sculptor starts by planning the big picture: Where do the different elements belong (things like the head, arms, torso, and feet), and how big should each one be? When we write CSS, we rough out the layout by pushing HTML tags around to create columns and a general layout for a page, making decisions along the way about elements like borders, widths, and dimensions.

After carving out the general form, the sculptor works in greater and greater detail on each section of the piece: introducing realistic details like wrinkles, folds in the skin, and muscle tone. With CSS, we slowly enhance the header, navigation, sidebar, footer, and so on with design treatments like color, gradients, typography, and shadows.

Finally, the sculptor preps the work for display, polishing and fine-tuning the overall composition. With CSS, we put finishing touches on our work as well: for instance, making sure it works for every visitor in every scenario, and that it loads fast.

In this chapter, we're finally going to start seeing how everything comes together in CSS by looking at the big picture. We're done with all the behind the scenes stuff and ready to make something that looks like a real Web page.

First Things First: Syntax

Ah yes, the funny characters. Just like the HTML we learned earlier in the book, CSS is a programming language with its own special syntax. It can be very forgiving, but we still need to learn the fundamentals.

You will remember in our first chapter that we looked at how easy CSS is to read and that I promised later to explain those funny characters. Well, it's time.

Consider this CSS rule:

```
p { color : white ; }
```

As you can imagine, this CSS rule tells us that every paragraph tag on the page should be white.

DON'T STRESS OVER THE VOCABULARY

I need to come clean: I had to look up these terms while writing this book. I've been writing CSS for a long time without knowing these things by heart. I mean, the language is familiar to me, and it should be familiar to you, too, but don't bother trying to memorize terms like *selector*, *property*, and *value*.

Instead, spend your brainpower recognizing the form and syntax. The first part identifies what we're targeting, and everything else goes inside squigglies. The colon connects the two things that describe what we're targeting, and the semicolon tells us we're done with that declaration and ready to describe the first part some more with another declaration.

TABLE 6.1 will help you understand what each character in the code block means.

TABLE 6.1   CSS Syntax Elements

CSS	ENGLISH
p	This first element is the *selector*. The selector tells us what type of item we're *selecting* to target with CSS. In our example, it's a familiar HTML abbreviation—p for paragraph—that targets every paragraph.
	Notice that it doesn't have any of the other special characters from HTML such as ‹ or ›. It's just the abbreviation. You can put almost anything in this spot: another HTML tag such as ‹div›, a class attribute from your HTML like .teaser, or an id attribute from your HTML such as #logo (the period and hash tag mean something, which I'll cover later).
{	This element is called many things—curly bracket, definite bracket, swirly bracket, and chicken lips (no, I did not make that up, check Wikipedia)—but I just call it a *squiggly*. This is an opening squiggly; you'll notice a closing squiggly to signify the end of this declaration. The CSS you write inside of these squigglies describes what your *selector* should look like.
color	This element is known as the *property*. Remember that in HTML we discussed attributes? Well, this element is very similar to an attribute; it defines what property of the selector we're about to describe. In this example, we're about to change the color of all paragraphs.
:	The *colon* connects the property and the value. In our example, it connects the property color and the specified value of white. It just needs to be between the property and the value—it doesn't matter whether you surround it with spaces or no spaces; it just needs to be on the same line.
white	This element is known as the *value* of the property. It describes what the property should look like. In our example, the value of the color property is white.
;	This *semicolon* tells us the declaration is over. You can add more declarations after this (a declaration is any property-and-value combination).
}	Finally, the closing squiggly as promised above. This indicates the end of a CSS rule.

Here's an example of a CSS rule with more than one declaration:

```
div{
  background-color: red;
  padding: 10px;
  }
```

This CSS rule tells us that every ‹div› tag should have a background-color value of red and 10 pixels of space around it.

Formatting Your CSS

A question that always comes up in my workshops, just as with HTML, is how much of the text formatting is required, versus how much of it is just personal preference?

TIP CSS doesn't require the final semicolon in a list of declarations, but I suggest you use it anyway because it's simpler to remember to end each declaration with a semicolon than to split each declaration with a semicolon. My bet is you'll make fewer mistakes when you follow simple rules like this.

All that's required by CSS is that each CSS rule begins with a selector and ends with one or more declarations surrounded by opening and closing squigglies. Inside the squigglies, each declaration must have a property and value separated by a colon, and a semicolon must separate declarations from each other.

Spaces and tabs are completely optional in CSS formatting. My suggestion is to write CSS for readability, keeping in mind that the most important thing is to be consistent with whatever style of formatting you choose.

FORMATTING IS LIKE FLOWING TEXT

I find that print designers often struggle with formatting. But with a little practice you'll begin to see formatting the same way you see typesetting long copy in a magazine. It's all about readability and consistency.

I usually write my selector and the opening squiggly on the first line. Then I go to the next line, tab in once, and write one declaration per line. Finally, I end with a closing squiggly on a line by itself, tabbed in the same as the declarations. If I'm feeling extra organized, I'll indent the entire CSS rule to match the nesting of the HTML. As an example, consider this HTML:

```
<div>
  <p>
    Durrr, you need to give us your email address to sign up for our
    email newsletter.
  </p>
</div>
```

Notice how the <p> tag is nested inside the <div> tag (FIGURE 6.1). I format my CSS like this to visually remind myself of the HTML structure I'm working with in my CSS file:

FIGURE 6.1
This illustrates simple
nested HTML.

```
div{
   background-color: red;
   padding: 10px;
   }


  p{
    color: white;
    }
```

But other ways of formatting are just as acceptable. Notice in the following example how there are no spaces and each rule is all on one line:

```
div{background-color:red;padding:10px}
p{color:white}
```

And here's another way to do it:

```
div
{
   background-color: red; padding: 10px
}


p
{
   color: white
}
```

In the end, the way you format your CSS is up to you. But I promise you will learn much faster and have fewer problems if you take the time to format cleanly and consistently.

White Space Increases File Size

One thing to note about your CSS formatting is that the more white space you use (the tabs, returns, and spaces), the larger the file size will be. Most of the time this isn't a big deal because the file sizes are very small and will download super fast anyway, which is why I recommend using extra white space to make your files more readable.

But with a very large Web site or a Web site that gets a lot of traffic, a bunch of very small files can add up and become costly for the company. That company would opt for the more compact CSS formatting.

For now, don't worry about it. Just know that your formatting decision *can* matter. Plus, you can sleep easy at night knowing that there are some hard-core developers on projects like this who can convert human-readable CSS to very compact, compressed CSS automatically and on the fly. If file size ever becomes an issue for you, you'll be reading a more advanced book by then anyway, so don't worry about it now.

Getting Fancy with Selectors

Let's take a look at a real-world example of some HTML and accompanying CSS—focusing on the *selector* part of the coding. Let's say we wanted to code the CSS for an error state for a contact form that wasn't filled out correctly (FIGURE 6.2). We might write our HTML like this:

FIGURE 6.2 This is what a typical error message might look like when a user doesn't fill out a Web form correctly.

Durrr, you need to give us your email address to sign up for our email newsletter.

```
<div id="form-message">
  <div class="error">
    <p>
      Durrr, you need to give us your email address to sign up for our
      ➥ email newsletter.
    </p>
  </div>
</div>
```

Hooking into CSS with class and id Attributes

In the CSS we have seen so far in this chapter, you'll notice I said we're targeting *every* <div> tag and <p> tag. This is great for broad, sweeping CSS declarations, but you'll often find yourself wanting to target just one little piece of your Web page, as in the preceding HTML example.

We can use class attributes and id attributes from our HTML as *hooks* that let us write CSS to control our HTML on a much more granular level. We'd write our CSS for the HTML in the preceding example like this:

```
#form-message{
  padding-top: 10px;
  border-top: 2px solid black;
  }

div.error{
  background-color: red;
  padding: 10px;
  }

div.error p{
  color: white;
  font-weight: bold;
  }
```

This might look a little more complex than what we've seen before because we've added a couple of funny characters—a period (.) and a hash (#)—and the selectors are more than just p. Don't worry, this is easy—let me walk you through it.

Combining Tags and Hooks

You can choose to be more specific with CSS by writing a selector that includes the class attribute or id attribute in addition to the tag itself. We do this by typing the tag you want to target and then stringing it together with a class attribute or id attribute. We string these together by connecting the period or hash with the tag, making sure to leave out any space characters.

Notice in the preceding code that we have a selector div.error with no spaces. This targets any <div> tag with a class attribute you have defined as error. In other words, it targets <div class="error">.

So div.error as a selector in CSS targets only <div class="error"> in HTML.

TIP The space character or lack of space character in selectors is actually very important, as opposed to spaces in the formatting, which don't matter.

The same would hold true for id attributes, but instead of using a period, you'd use a hash (div#form-message).

TABLE 6.2 shows some examples of how CSS targets HTML.

TABLE 6.2 Using CSS to Target HTML

	div	.error	div.error	p.error
<div>	✔			
<div class="error">	✔	✔	✔	
<p class="error">		✔		✔
<span class="error">		✔		

The check marks indicate where a CSS selector would match an HTML tag. Where there's no check mark, the CSS would not take effect.

Notice that when we reference only the HTML tag (when we want our CSS to apply to every tag of a certain type) in CSS, the selectors are not prepended with any funny characters such as a period or hash.

Targeting Nested HTML

Let's say you only want to target a <p> tag that's nested inside <div class="error"> (FIGURE 6.3). CSS gives us a simple way of doing this; we just need to build on what we've already learned.

FIGURE 6.3
We're getting a little more specific with our CSS selectors.

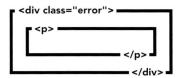

In CSS, you can target HTML by the way it's nested, in addition to the tag name, class attribute, and id attribute. The first part of the selector targets the parent tag, and each chunk of text that follows (with a space before it) is nested in the parent tag prior to it. Wow, that's a mouthful. Let's see how our nested HTML matches up with some simple CSS selectors (FIGURE 6.4).

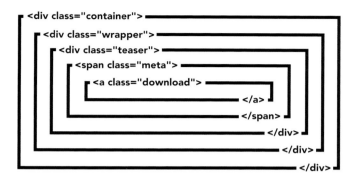

FIGURE 6.4
With HTML you can nest
things as much (or as
little) as you need.

You can get as fancy with this as you want.

```
<div class="container">
  <div class="wrapper">
    <div class="teaser">
      <span class="meta">(PDF, 1 Megabyte) </span>
      <a href="annual-report.pdf" class="download">Download Now</a>
    </div>
  </div>
</div>
```

You could target the link in this example several ways.

The easiest way would be to target .download, which would find anything with a class of download. That code would look like this:

```
.download{
  font-weight: bold;
  color: red;
  }
```

But let's say you want to target only links with a class attribute of download inside a <div> tag with a class attribute of teaser. You'd target div.teaser .download to do this:

```
div.teaser .download{
  font-weight: bold;
  color: red;
  }
```

You could even go crazy and target the link with a selector like this:

```
div.container div.wrapper div.teaser a.download{
  font-weight: bold;
  color: red;
  }
```

Usually this is a little extreme, but occasionally I'll have to do something like this when I'm working on a larger site I didn't code originally and I want to make sure my CSS rule doesn't affect other parts of the site. In that case, being overly specific can be helpful.

Reading Selectors in Plain English

An exercise I find helpful when I'm trying to follow a complex selector is to read it in plain English. Here's a really hard one (FIGURE 6.5):

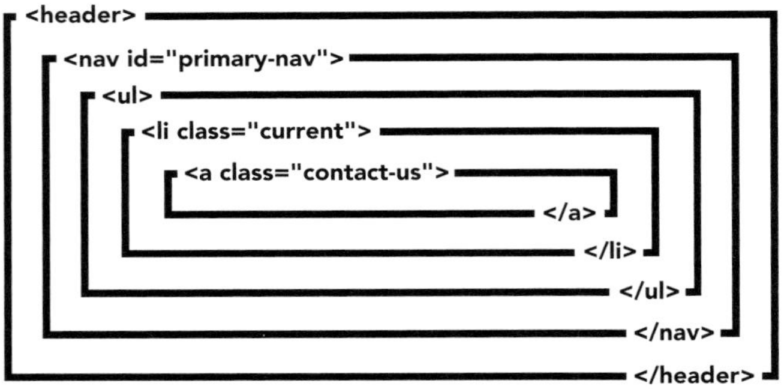

FIGURE 6.5
This illustrates a common way navigation is marked up with HTML.

```
header nav#primary-nav ul li.current a.contact-us{
  font-weight: bold;
}
```

In this example, we want something to be bold, but what exactly do we want to be bold?

We find out by reading the CSS backwards. I'm inserting line breaks like in a poem to make the CSS easier to read. So, reading from the end of the line to the beginning:

We're targeting an <a> tag with a class attribute of contact-us

¬ that's inside an <li> tag with a class attribute of current

¬ that's inside a <ul> tag

¬ that's inside a <nav> tag that has an id attribute of primary-nav

¬ that's inside a <header> tag.

TIP When you read your CSS as I'm describing, it just has to be a true statement when comparing it with the HTML. Your selector doesn't have to include every tag in the nested hierarchy.

Checking and Double-Checking Your Selectors

If any part of your selector doesn't match up exactly with the HTML, the CSS rule will not take effect.

There are two lessons here:

- CSS is very powerful because you can design your CSS selectors to be super specific.

- The more complicated your CSS selectors get, the easier it is to make a mistake and the more likely you are to get frustrated because your selectors aren't working the way you think they should.

With great power comes great responsibility. Since you're a beginner, my suggestion is to create simple selectors. As you get more comfortable skimming CSS and making sense of it, you'll know when it's okay to make some really complicated selectors.

Commenting Your CSS

You already know how HTML allows you to comment on your work to communicate with fellow coders and remind yourself what you're doing. CSS gives us a way to write comments, too. The syntax is a little different, though, so you need to keep things straight. Here's how you add comments with CSS:

```
/* Your comment goes here */
```

You begin a CSS comment with a slash and an asterisk. You end the comment in reverse order with an asterisk and then a slash. The browser will ignore anything that you put inside the asterisks. Here's an example:

```
/*
bigger text for intro paragraphs - multiline comment
*/
.entry p.teaser{
  font-size: 24px;
  color: green; /* need to change this to the brand-standard hex value
  ➥ before we go live */
  /* changed the line-height so the bigger text does not look squished */
  line-height: 30px;
  }
```

Normally, you wouldn't need to comment this much in your CSS. I'm just showing you different ways to format comments. You can put comments anywhere you want, just don't break your CSS syntax.

Let's Write Some CSS

We've spent a lot of time building up to this moment. We've learned how to write HTML that gives meaning and structure to your content. We've learned the funny characters and syntax of HTML and CSS, breaking down what seems to be very complex into bite-sized chunks. The rest of the way, my friends, is all downhill.

When I start writing CSS for a Web site, it helps me to think in terms of the types of CSS I'm writing. While there's no technical distinction that sets this forth, I've found it makes my job a lot easier to identify the categories of look and feel that CSS controls:

- Typography
- Layout
- Interaction (for instance, rollover effects)

Setting Type with CSS

Print designers and Web designers alike geek out over typography. It's universal. Don't act like you (or at least one of your designer friends) don't have a Helvetica coffee mug sitting on your desk right now.

Heck, the love of typography even rubs off on our families, who like to impress us by naming the fonts they use in their email signatures and interoffice memos at work. They try to make fun of Comic Sans with us, even if their heart's not in it.

As a print designer, typography will be by far one of the easiest things for you to pick up when you start writing CSS by hand. So let's dive right in. With simple CSS, here are a few of the details we can control with typography:

- Font choice
- Font size
- Font weight
- Color
- Leading
- Kerning
- Case of the letters (all uppercase, all lowercase, and mixed case)

Selecting a Font

You already know how you need a font installed on your computer for it to work when you import an InDesign project. Typography on the Web works the same way. The problem is, it's not realistic or legal for us to prompt users to install fonts on their computers.

That's why there are "Web-safe" fonts like Verdana, Georgia, and Times New Roman. These fonts are on most everyone's computer already, so it's a safe bet that if we use CSS to specify that font, it'll be there on the visitor's computer and the page will display as expected.

Just to be safe, though, we need to write our CSS in a way so that there's a backup font or font type, just in case someone doesn't have the font we specify first.

> **SPECIFYING SPECIAL FONTS**
>
> Some recent innovations in technology and font licensing let us specify fonts that aren't permanently installed on a visitor's computer. The font we specify is installed temporarily on our visitor's system so they can see the design the way we want them to. Visit cssforprintdesigners.com/web-typography to see what options are available and to learn more.

We specify a font by using the font-family property.

```
h2{
  font-family: helvetica, arial, sans-serif;
  }
```

We can specify any fonts we want in the string after the colon, as long as a comma and a space separate each one. The visitor's computer is going to try and find the first font on the system. If it finds it, it uses it; if not, it moves on to the next font in your list, and so on. Finally, you can specify a font-type like serif or sans-serif for a worst-case fallback in case the user's computer doesn't have any of the fonts you specify.

You will sometimes see a font-family declaration like this:

```
h2{
  font-family: "Helvetica Neue", helvetica, arial, sans-serif;
  }
```

 TIP As with all CSS properties we'll be looking at, the property must be typed exactly as it's shown. It needs to remain lowercase, the hyphen (if one exists) is required, and there can be no errant spaces.

The only difference between this code and the preceding example is that one of the fonts is surrounded by double tick marks. If the font you're specifying has a space in the name, you need to put double tick marks around it. Notice that the comma is outside the tick marks.

Selecting Units of Measurement

We can't get much further without talking about units of measurement on the Web. There are several units of measurement for Web designers to select from, just like in print. You're used to seeing inches, picas, and centimeters. These units of measurement are literal measurements and are the same no matter what ruler you're using.

Units on the Web are a little different. You have several options for units of measurement on the Web, from percentage to pixels to ems. Percentages are just what they sound like, pixels are the size of the pixel on your user's screen, ems are a relative unit of measurement. For the most part, it's safe to use pixels, so I recommend that you start there.

THE POWERFUL EM

You have probably never heard of the em before, and that's okay.

One em is equal to the current font size, so that makes it a relative unit of measurement. It takes a little math to understand, so here's a simple example: If your font starts equivalent to 12px and you tell it to be 1.5em, the font size becomes equivalent to 18px because 12 x 1.5 = 18.
The em can become very useful to you when you want things to scale relatively. For example, you might want to set the width of an object to be relative to its font size.

There is no need to learn how the em works now; just keep this unit of measurement in your back pocket.

Changing Font Size

We set the size of a font online using the font-size property:

```
h2{
    font-family: "Helvetica Neue", helvetica, arial, sans-serif;
    font-size: 18px;
    }
```

You can use any value with any unit of measurement here. You just need to make sure your unit of measurement is connected to the number without any spaces.

Setting Font Weight

We use the font-weight property to set a font to be bold or regular:

```
h2{
  font-family: "Helvetica Neue", helvetica, arial, sans-serif;
  font-size: 18px;
  font-weight: bold;
  }
```

Setting Font Style

We us the font-style property to set a font to be normal or italic:

```
h2{
  font-family: "Helvetica Neue", helvetica, arial, sans-serif;
  font-size: 18px;
  font-weight: bold;
  font-style: italic;
  }
```

Tweaking the Color

You are a print designer, so you know all about color. Being the smart person that you are, you probably know what hexadecimal values are— you know, the funny-looking six-character definitions for Web colors with a hash tag in front of them? These days we're not constrained to using only Web-safe colors, so any hexadecimal value is fair game (**FIGURE 6.6**).

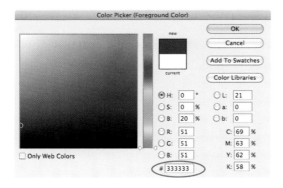

FIGURE 6.6
Photoshop's Color Picker makes it easy to find hexadecimal (or RGB) values.

We set the color of type online using the color property:

```
h2{
    font-family: "Helvetica Neue", helvetica, arial, sans-serif;
    font-size: 18px;
    font-weight: bold;
    font-style: italic;
    color: #333333;
}
```

USING HEXADECIMAL SHORTHAND

As you get more familiar with CSS and look at other designers' work, you will occasionally see a shorter hexadecimal code like #333 or #DDD or #069. That's just a way to write the same thing with fewer characters. Here's how that works: If the first two, middle two, or last two characters of the full six-character code match, you can shorten your value by writing the corresponding character just once. In other words, #006699 becomes #069.

You can use other values besides hexadecimals. For example, you can use RGB values, which are formatted like this: rgb(200, 54, 54). I use hexadecimal values, but either one is fine if you have a preference.

Changing the Line Height

Using line-height with CSS is the same thing as adjusting the leading in print design. That is to say, this property sets the vertical space that a line of text takes up (FIGURE 6.7).

FIGURE 6.7 Don't forget to take line-height into account when you're designing for the Web.

```
line-height: 24px; ──── Leading and line-height are equal to the
    font-size: 18px; ──── vertical space taken up by a line of text.
```

We set the leading using the line-height property:

```
h2{
    font-family: "Helvetica Neue", helvetica, arial, sans-serif;
    font-size: 18px;
    font-weight: bold;
    font-style: italic;
    color: #333;
    line-height: 24px;
}
```

Just like with font-size, you can use any value and unit of measurement here. In our example, the value is 24 and the unit of measurement is pixels, or px.

Kerning with CSS

CSS doesn't give you as much control as Adobe Illustrator or InDesign when it comes to kerning, but it does give you a rough tool to use in the letter-spacing property. I say "rough" because CSS kerns the entire string of characters in the tag you specify, and because the units of measurement are not nearly as precise, due to the limitations of the pixels on a screen.

We use the letter-spacing property to control the horizontal spacing between each letter in a string of text:

```
h2{
  font-family: "Helvetica Neue", helvetica, arial, sans-serif;
  font-size: 18px;
  font-weight: bold;
  font-style: italic;
  color: #333;
  font-size: 18px;
  line-height: 24px;
  letter-spacing: -1px;
  }
```

You can use any unit of measurement or value in this spot, including a negative value if you want to kern the letters in tighter on each other.

Setting ALL UPPERCASE, all lowercase, and Mixed Case

CSS lets you change the case of the text in the HTML very easily with the text-transform property:

```
h2{
  font-family: "Helvetica Neue", helvetica, arial, sans-serif;
  font-size: 18px;
  font-weight: bold;
  font-style: italic;
  color: #333;
  font-size: 18px;
  line-height: 24px;
  letter-spacing: -1px;
  text-transform: uppercase;
  }
```

The values can to choose from are uppercase, capitalize, and lowercase. As with most CSS, you can tell it to lose any inherited CSS by declaring none as the value.

DON'T USE ALL CAPS IN YOUR HTML

If your site's look and feel calls for an ALL-CAPS (or all uppercase) head-line, there's no need to type it that way in the HTML. Just write it so it's properly title cased. You can use CSS to transform the text later.

Laying Out a Web Page

When a print designer lays out a spread in a magazine, it means she's bringing in imagery, wrapping text, creating columns, making gutters, and defining spaces with graphic treatments like borders. Web design is the same way, but instead of doing it with a page layout program like InDesign, we use CSS to push HTML tags around.

Wrapping Text with Floats

If you want an image to have text wrapping, you can use CSS to float it to the left or right. Simply telling an image to float: right; or float: left; will do the trick.

Also, you'll want to make sure there's some margin around the sides of the image the text might bump up against. For an image that's floated to the left, that means adding margin to the right side (as well as, potentially, the top and bottom). For an image that's floating right, it means you'll want to add margin to the left side (FIGURE 6.8).

FIGURE 6.8 When you float an image to wrap text around it, don't forget to add margin to the image so the text doesn't butt up against it too closely.

Here's the HTML:

```
<img class="headshot" src="images/ceo-headshot.jpg" alt="Our CEO" />
<p>
  Our beloved CEO has years of experience telling us what to do and not
  following through on his own commitments. He is a micromanager, but
  not an annoying one. We sort of like him for his antics in front of
  clients, and he is endearing when he drags in each morning at 11:00
  after a quick nine holes and a six pack of imported beer.
</p>
```

And here's the CSS:

```
img{
  float: right;
  margin-left: 10px;
  margin-bottom: 10px;
  }
```

Floating for Layout

Most Web designs call for columns to be part of the layout, but CSS doesn't have a way to say, "I want to make a column." So we use floats instead. When we want to make columns in our layout, we use CSS to "float" tags to the left or right just like we did with the image example in the preceding section. Consider the following HTML (FIGURE 6.9):

FIGURE 6.9 This is what our HTML looks like before we write any CSS.

```
<div class="wrap">
  <div class="main">
    Make this the left column.
  </div>
  <div class="side">
    Make this the right column.
  </div>
</div>
```

Creating columns is a three-step process.

1. Set the width. If you don't set a width for the boxes, floating usually won't do any good—and besides, what good is a column that goes the entire width of a page (FIGURE 6.10)?

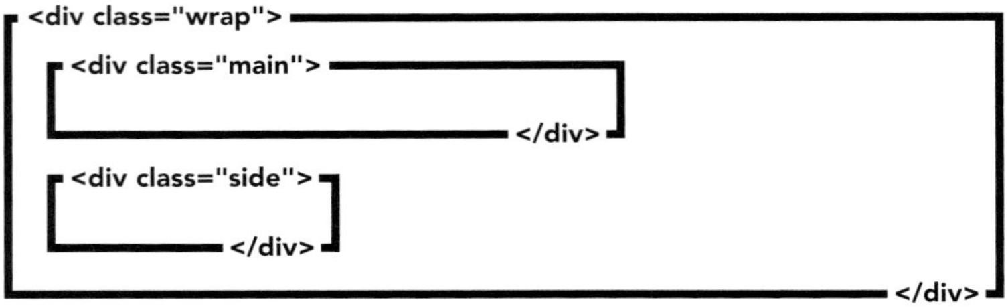

FIGURE 6.10 This is what happens when we set a width for each of the columns we're about to create.

```
.wrap{
  width: 960px;
  }

  .main{
    width: 760px;
    }

  .side{
    width: 200px;
    }
```

2. Set the floats. We use the float property to tell the <div> tags to float left and right (FIGURE 6.11):

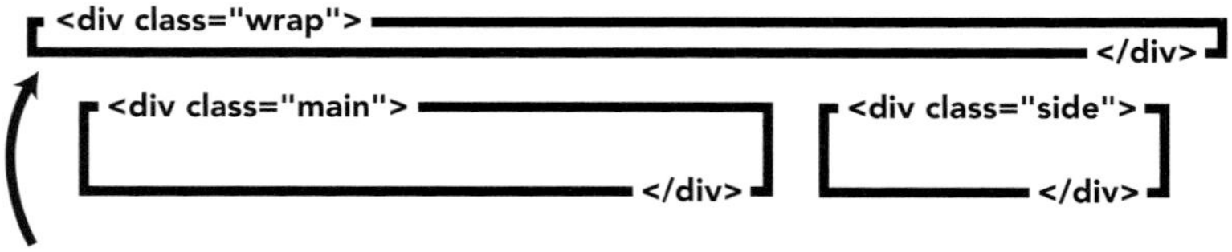

FIGURE 6.11 When we float children tags, the parent tag collapses on itself. Don't ask why, it just does.

```
.wrap{
  width: 960px;
  }

  .main{
    width: 760px;
```

```
        float: left;
        }

    .side{
        width: 200px;
        float: right;
        }
```

Notice that this step causes something odd to happen. The parent container <div class="wrap"> is not surrounding the nested boxes any more—it just collapses on itself. Since 99.9 percent of the time you will want the parent box to encapsulate its children, we need to know how to fix this.

3. Clear your floats. To fix the problem introduced in step 2, we have to do what's called clearing floats (FIGURE 6.12). The simplest method that works most of the time is to set the overflow property *of the parent element* to hidden like this:

FIGURE 6.12 Once we clear our floats, the parent tag encapsulates its children once more.

```
.wrap{
    width: 960px;
    overflow: hidden;
    }

    .main{
        width: 760px;
        float: left;
        }

    .side{
        width: 200px;
        float: right;
        }
```

I wish I had a good reason to share with you why we have to clear floats, but there's not one—it's just something we have to live with.

 TIP There are many ways to clear floats; I have described just one technique. To learn more, check out cssforprintdesigners.com/ clearing-floats.

Getting Fancy with Floats

If you have a series of tags and you float them in the same direction, they will float beside each other (FIGURE 6.13). This specification would be useful if you wanted to make a three-column layout, for example.

FIGURE 6.13 If you float three tags to the left, you can make a simple three-column layout.

TIP It's very common for Web designers to create horizontal navigation by floating a series of <li> tags to the left.

TIP When you float a block-level element, it automatically starts acting like an inline element, so it will take up as little horizontal space as possible.

TIP In print design, we refer to the space between columns of text as gutters. In Web design, we typically create this type of spacing with padding or margin.

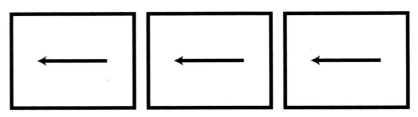

Spacing with Border, Padding, and Margin

When we specify the border, padding, or margin property in our CSS, it adds to the width of a tag, which causes us to have to use math when we design, which can be a hassle. It's easy to tell when a beginner is responsible for the PSD I'm coding because the border, padding, and margin properties will be irregular and inconsistent.

Adding this spacing drives CSS coders crazy, and it will soon drive you crazy as well. When you want to put space between objects in your designs, everything is much simpler when you use round numbers.

Let's say you have a two-column layout with an overall width of 960 pixels (FIGURE 6.14). The main column needs to add up to 760 pixels, and the sidebar column needs to total 200 pixels. That's easy, because 760 + 200 = 960. It will fit.

FIGURE 6.14
The children both add up to 960 pixels, so they will fit inside a 960-pixel parent tag.

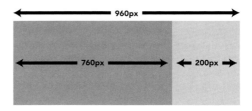

But add any amount of width to either of the interior columns with a border, padding, or margin property, and your layout will break because the total width of the interior columns is greater than the parent (FIGURE 6.15). If you add a 10-pixel border to the sidebar, the total width of the sidebar becomes 210 pixels. And 970 total pixels will not fit inside 960 pixels.

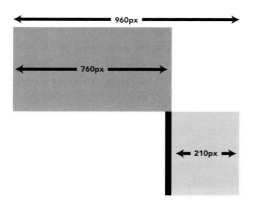

FIGURE 6.15 When you add any amount of width, the children add up to over 960 pixels, so they don't fit inside their parent tag any more.

When a floated object doesn't have room to float up next to another object, it just drops down to the next line. Take a look at how the overall width of a simple object changes when you add border, padding, and margin to it in increments of 10 pixels (FIGURE 6.16). Then try to imagine how much fun this would be if you had a three- or four-column layout with 2 pixels of border here, 6 pixels of margin there, and so on. It can get ugly real fast.

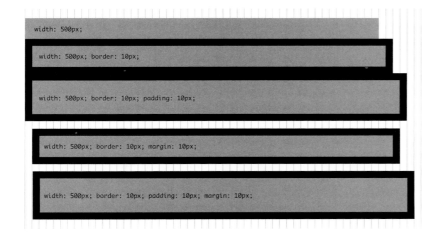

FIGURE 6.16 Border, padding, and margin make us do math. Which sucks.

There are two key takeaways here:

- Keep it simple. We're all designers here, not mathematicians.
- If something seems to be pushed down below where it belongs (as in Figure 6.15), check the combined width by adding up the width declared for your object, as well as the width added by border, padding, and margin on the left and right sides of your tag. Odds are, you have tried to squish too much width into too small a space.

Setting Borders

We set borders for a tag using the border property. Here's an example:

```
nav{
  border: 5px solid #000;
  }
```

This CSS will set a solid border of 5 pixels on all four sides of the <nav> tag (FIGURE 6.17).

FIGURE 6.17 This tag has 5 pixels of a solid black border on all sides.

If you prefer to have more control over your borders than setting the border to be the same on all sides, you also have the following properties, starting clockwise from the top (keep this clockwise order in mind; you're going to learn something fun in a moment): border-top, border-right, border-bottom, and border-left. If you leave one of these out, your element won't have a border on that side.

If you want a thick dark line at the bottom of your navigation area and a thin gray line at the top of your navigation area, but nothing on either side (FIGURE 6.18), you might write your CSS like this:

```
nav{
  border-bottom: 5px solid #000;
  border-top: 1px solid #DDD;
  }
```

FIGURE 6.18 This tag has 5 pixels of a solid black border on the bottom and 1 pixel of a solid light gray border on the top. It doesn't have any border on either the left or right side.

Notice we're putting three separate values in the value area of the CSS rule:

- The first is the thickness, or width, of the border (in our example 5 pixels and 1 pixel, respectively).

- The second is the style of border (solid).

- The third is the color (#000 and #DDD).

   You'll want to leave these values in this order and separate each with a single space, keeping them all on the same line.

Setting the Style of Borders

If instead of a solid border, you wanted a dotted border, or a dashed border, or a double border, you can create that as well (FIGURE 6.19):

```
nav{
  border-bottom: 5px solid #000;
  border-top: 1px dotted #DDD;
  }
```

FIGURE 6.19 We've changed the border on the top from solid to dotted.

MORE BORDER STYLES

There are a lot more border styles available to use, though I rarely use anything other than solid or dotted. As with the rest of this book, I'm covering only the most-used stuff and giving you what you need to find the rest online. Just Google "CSS border-style" if you want the full list.

Inheriting Border Color

If you don't declare a color, the element will inherit the color property set by its parent tag. You'll learn more about this phenomenon (called, smartly, *inheritance*) in a later chapter.

Adding Padding

We use the padding property to add space that butts up against the border on the *inside* of a tag.

As with the border property, you can set the padding for all four sides of a tag, like this:

```
nav{
  border-bottom: 5px solid #000;
  border-top: 1px dotted #DDD;
  padding: 20px;
  }
```

Or you can go crazy and set a different padding for each of the four sides with the following properties (notice they work just like the border as discussed earlier, clockwise starting with the top): padding-top, padding-right, padding-bottom, and padding-left.

```
nav{
  border-bottom: 5px solid #000;
  border-top: 1px dotted #DDD;
  padding-top: 20px;
  padding-bottom: 15px;
}
```

Since the padding is on the inside of the border, if you set a background color for the tag, it will fill in behind the padding all the way up against the border (FIGURE 6.20).

```
nav{
  border-bottom: 5px solid #000;
  border-top: 1px dotted #DDD;
  padding-top: 20px;
  padding-bottom: 15px;
  background-color: #EEE;
}
```

FIGURE 6.20 We've added some padding so it gets taller, and we've added a gray background-color.

Setting Margins

The margin property is similar to padding, in that it also butts up against the border. The difference is that the margin is the space on the *outside* of the border, not the inside. When you set a background color, it doesn't fill in behind the margin because it's outside the border.

You set margin the exact same way you do padding—that is, you can set the margin on all four sides with the margin property, or you can set the margins individually for each side with margin-top, margin-right, margin-bottom, and margin-left.

```
nav{
  border-bottom: 5px solid #000;
  border-top: 1px dotted #DDD;
  padding-top: 20px;
  padding-bottom: 15px;
  background-color: #EEE;
  margin-top: 10px;
  margin-right: 20px;
```

```
    margin-bottom: 30px;
    margin-left: 40px;
    }
```

As you can see, this coding is all very simple, but it takes a lot of typing. If only there were a way to shorten this CSS rule a little bit. But wait, there is!

Using CSS Shorthand for Padding and Margins

When you start writing CSS as we've been doing here, it can become very wordy. CSS shorthand gives us a way to accomplish the same thing with fewer keystrokes.

The padding and margin properties share the same shorthand, so we can kill two birds with one stone. Remember how I told you earlier to pay attention to the fact that we were starting the padding and margin properties at the top and working our way clockwise?

With padding, starting at the top and going clockwise for each side of the tag, we have padding-top, padding-right, padding-bottom, and padding-left. And you remember margin works the same way.

Take a look at this CSS:

```
div{
    padding-top: 10px;
    padding-right: 20px;
    padding-bottom: 30px;
    padding-left: 40px;
    }
```

CSS shorthand lets us write that CSS like this instead:

```
div{
    padding: 10px 20px 30px 40px;
    }
```

You just start typing the first measurement from the top and work your way around the tag clockwise. We can take this a step further if your top and bottom match, as well as your left and right sides. For example, you might want to write something like this:

```
div{
    padding-top: 0;
    padding-right: 20px;
    padding-bottom: 0;
    padding-left: 20px;
    }
```

 TIP I've actually already given you the shorthand for border. I didn't bother telling you earlier though, because the longhand for border is harder to memorize than the shorthand, and I don't see the value in learning the hard way when you can learn the easy way.

 TIP Notice that the value 0 doesn't need a unit of measurement because zero means zero no matter what unit it's in.

Notice how the top and bottom are both 0 and the left and right are both 20px. You could write this shorthand:

```
div{
  padding: 0 20px;
  }
```

This CSS zeroes out the padding for the top and bottom and sets the left and right sides both to 20 pixels.

Using Margins to Center Tags

If you want to center your layout in Web design, you do that by setting the margin on the right and left of a tag to auto and declaring a width for the tag. There are several ways to do this:

```
margin: 10px auto 5px auto;
margin: 0 auto;
margin: auto;
```

Removing Default Spacing with a CSS Reset

All this math can get pretty frustrating under tight deadlines. Eventually you're going to add space to something and the math won't add up. You'll end up scratching your head, wondering what's wrong. This is a good time to think about CSS resets.

In Chapter 5, you learned that when you write HTML without any CSS, it reads like a Word doc. That's because every browser applies default CSS to HTML files so they're readable—there's already CSS telling your Web page to look that way before you ever write any CSS. This default CSS controls the size of your heading tags and paragraph text, the spacing above and below your headings, paragraphs and lists, and much more.

The problem is every browser disagrees a little bit about exactly how much space and what font sizes to use. You can override the default CSS by writing your own CSS, but that can become laborious. To get around this, some pretty smart CSS developers came up with the idea of resetting the default CSS from browsers by overriding it with a reset style sheet (FIGURE 6.21) that they reuse on every project.

I've compiled some additional pointers and a list of CSS resets you can use in your own projects at cssforprintdesigners.com/css-reset.

With a CSS reset like this, every browser is instructed to agree on how much spacing there should be around each tag, how big each font should be, and a few other things. What you need to know is this: I recommend you start your projects with a CSS reset because it will make your math work much better.

FIGURE 6.21 With a CSS reset, default spacing and font sizes are replaced with consistent font sizes and spacing.

Designing for Interaction

A lot of folks out there think print designers don't really understand interactivity, but that's just not true. I know from being a print designer and from talking with print designers all over the country. As a matter of fact, I believe print designers understand interaction better than a lot of Web designers.

Think about a fancy fold brochure. Your "users" literally interact with the piece, discovering its contents through exploration, uncovering more and more the longer they engage with it. Environmental graphics are the most interactive of all—customers literally walk around them, interacting with something from all angles, taking in the message based on the way it's designed.

So yes, print designers get interactivity.

But often a print designer who has designed a Web site creates interactive *features* like hover effects and drop-down menus that end up feeling awkward. I think the reason for this is more a lack of understanding of the tools of interactivity on the Web than it is a lack of understanding of the principles of interaction. As print designers, we're used to creating interactions in the physical world—placement matters, how it feels in your hands matters.

When you're designing for interaction on a Web site, the screen and the mouse are the tools people use to explore things, so we need to find new ways to achieve interaction so it feels natural, physical, and responsive.

There aren't physical pages to turn on the Internet—just metaphors for pages. So Web designers have to come up with ways to let users of a Web site know that something is hidden behind an interaction.

We do this two ways:

• First, we make things look clickable. That's why buttons on Web sites often look like the buttons we see in real life: They often look slightly raised with a sense of depth, and their appearance changes when they're clicked.

• Second, before something is clicked, Web designers need to give users some indication that the element can be clicked. This helps users understand that they should try clicking it to see what happens.

Using Interactive CSS Commands

Before you can begin thinking about adding interactivity to your Web site, you need to know what tools you have at your disposal. CSS provides a simple way to tell the objects on our Web pages how to behave when the user rolls over them and clicks them with the mouse.

You learned above about creating selectors to target your HTML tags and change their appearance. Now, we will add a final layer to our CSS selectors, for interactivity.

It's as simple as adding a colon to a selector and appending a word to it. There are just a few words to pick from, so this is pretty simple. TABLE 6.3 shows you what your options are, and what they do.

TABLE 6.3 Interactive CSS Commands

CSS	ENGLISH
a:hover	Use this command to tell your CSS what something should look like when a user rolls over it with the mouse. It's useful for letting your users know when they can interact with something.
a:active	Use this command to tell your CSS what something should look like while your user is clicking a link with the mouse. It's useful for making buttons or links look like they're being pressed down.
a:visited	Use this command to tell your CSS what something should look like after a user has clicked it. It's useful in long lists of links where you want your users to know what links they have already clicked.

TIP You don't have to use each of these interactive CSS commands every time you want to design interaction. You can pick and choose which ones to use. For example, in main navigation I usually don't bother with the :visited state.

In Table 6.3 you will notice I am using the <a> tag as an example. You can use these interactive CSS commands for other tags, class attributes, and id attributes as well. The problem is that not all browsers recognize these commands on all tags, but they all recognize them on <a> tags, so you're OK sticking with <a> tags for now.

MORE VOCABULARY YOU DON'T NEED TO MEMORIZE

These interactive CSS commands have a complicated sounding label to describe them. They're known as pseudo-selectors. I'm not telling you this because I want you to learn how to pronounce it or because you need to memorize this term to code a Web site. I bring it up because as you become more mature in your Web coding, you'll eventually come across it in more advanced online tutorials and Web design blogs, and I want you to know what it is, that's all.

Let's take a look at a couple examples of how to use these interactive CSS commands.

In this example, we're telling all <a> tags to start out set to blue.

```
a{
   color: blue;
   }
```

When the user rolls over the link, let's change color to black to give the user an indication that it's something that can be clicked.

```
a{
   color: blue;
   }

a:hover{
   color: black;
   }
```

Now, while the user is pressing the mouse button on the link, let's reverse the text out by making the background color change to black and the color of the text change to white. This change confirms for the user that he or she has hit the target and that something is about to happen.

```
a{
   color: blue;
   }

a:hover{
   color: black;
   }

a:active{
   background-color: black;
   color: white;
   }
```

And finally, after the user has clicked the link, let's turn it gray to give the user an indication that he or she has already been there. Next time the user returns to this page and sees that link, it'll be gray.

```css
a{
  color: blue;
  }

a:hover{
  color: black;
  }

a:active{
  background-color: black;
  color: white;
  }

a:visited{
  color: gray;
  }
```

Let's Make a Web Page Together

Believe it or not, you have learned enough CSS just following along in this chapter to create a simple Web page layout (FIGURE 6.22). By now the funny characters should not be as confusing. They may still take a little more time to read than plain English, and that's fine. Read through the code carefully, especially the comments in the CSS.

FIGURE 6.22
This shows a simple two-column layout you can make with everything you have learned in this chapter.

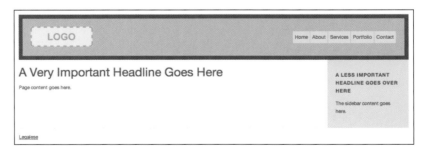

Here's the HTML for a simple Web page:

```html
<header>
  <img src="images/logo.gif" alt="Company logo" />
  <nav>
```

```
    <ul>
      <li>
        <a href="index.html">Home</a>
      </li>
      <li>
        <a href="about.html">About</a>
      </li>
       <li>
        <a href="services.html">Services</a>
      </li>
       <li>
        <a href="portfolio.html">Portfolio</a>
      </li>
      <li>
        <a href="contact.html">Contact</a>
      </li>
    </ul>
  </nav>
</header>
<div id="content">
  <div class="main">
    <h1>
      A Very Important Headline Goes Here
    </h1>
    <p>
      Page content goes here.
    </p>
  </div>
  <div class="side">
    <h2>
      A Less Important Headline Goes Over Here
    </h2>
    <p>
      The sidebar content goes here.
    </p>
  </div>
</div>
<footer>
  <p>
    <a href="legalese.html">Legalese</a>
  </p>
</footer>
```

And here's the CSS:

```css
header{
  background-color: #BBB; /* medium gray color */
  width: 900px; /* we want the overall width to be 960, so we're going to
  ➥ do some math with border and padding next */
  padding: 20px; /* 20 on all four sides means we are adding 40 to the
  ➥ overall width. 900 + 40 = 940 */
  border: 10px solid; /* this adds 20 total to the overall width.
  ➥ 940 + 20 = 960 */
  margin: auto; /* centers header */
  font-family: "Helvetica Neue", helvetica, arial, sans-serif;
  ➥ /* selecting a font for header and everything inside it */
  font-size: 12px;
  line-height: 20px;
  color: #444; /* dark gray color for text and border */
  overflow: hidden; /* planning ahead to clear floats */
}

header img{
  float: left;
}

nav ul{
  overflow: hidden; /* planning ahead to clear floats */
  padding: 0;
  float: right;
}

nav li{
  float: left; /* float every <li> tag to the left, so they stack
  ➥ in order */
}

nav a{
  display: block; /* this is required for the padding on the next
  ➥ line to work */
  padding: 5px; /* put some spacing around the links */
  margin-right: 1px; /* put a pixel of space between each link */
  background-color: #DDD; /* light gray background color */
  color: #444; /* dark gray text color */
  text-decoration: none; /* gets rid of the default underline
  ➥ on links */
}
```

```
    nav a:hover{
       background-color: #FFF; /* white */
       color: #000; /* black */
       }

    nav a:active{
       margin-top: 1px; /* nudges down the nav item by one pixel when
       ➥ it is pressed */
       }

#content{
   overflow: hidden; /* again, planning ahead to clear floats */
   width: 960px; /* matches the width of header above */
   margin: auto; /* centers #content */
   font-family: "Helvetica Neue", helvetica, arial, sans-serif; /*
   ➥ selecting a font for #content and everything inside it */
   font-size: 12px;
   line-height: 20px;
   color: #444; /* dark gray color for text and border */
   }

   .main{
      width: 740px;
      padding-right: 20px; /* 740 + 20 = 760 */
      float: left;
      }

   h1{
      font-size: 30px; /* big headline */
      font-weight: normal; /* headlines come bold by default, so we set
      ➥ it to normal if we want */
      }

   .side{
      width: 160px;
      padding: 20px; /* 760 + 160 + 40 = 960 so it fits! */
      float: right;
      background-color: #DDD;
      }

   h2{
      font-size: 12px;
      text-transform: uppercase;
      letter-spacing: 1px;
      }
```

```
footer{
    border-top:1px dotted #DDD; /* subtly separate footer from #content
    ➥ visually */
    width: 960px; /* matches the width of header and #content */
    margin: auto; /* centers footer */
    font-family: "Helvetica Neue", helvetica, arial, sans-serif; /*
    ➥ selecting a font for footer and everything inside it */
    font-size: 12px;
    line-height: 20px;
    color: #444; /* dark gray color for text and border */
    }
```

You Already Know a Lot

Download the video clips for this book from **www.peachpit.com/ cssforprintdesigners** (Register at the site.)

You just looked at 90 percent of a completed Web design project. It's not pretty, and the content is just placeholder text, but you did it! TABLE 6.4 provides a list of all the CSS we just learned.

TABLE 6.4 CSS Properties

CSS	ENGLISH
font-family	This is how we pick our font.
font-size	This is how we pick our font size.
font-weight	This is how we choose bold or normal for a font.
font-style	This is how we choose italic or regular for a font.
color	This is how we pick the color.
text-decoration	This is how we control underlines.
width	This is how we set the width of something.
border	This is how we set the border for something.
padding	The space on the inside of a border.
margin	The space on the outside of a border.
background-color	This is how we pick the background color.
overflow	We set this to auto to clear floats.
float	This is how we wrap text around images, make columns, and create horizontal navigation.

The last 10 percent, discussed over the next few chapters, is where you get to have some fun, putting the finishing touches on your work of art now that you have the overall structure mocked up.

7

Designing
with CSS

*How to Make Your Layouts Pop
with Images and CSS3*

ONE THING THAT always impresses me when I watch print designers work (or any designer for that matter) is how every single one of us uses our design tools in different ways to achieve our creative vision.

When you take any powerful tool and put it in the hands of someone with a creative mind, that person will find new ways to do things. That's the wonderful thing about tools—when they're fully comprehended, there are no limits to what can be accomplished. All it takes is a little imagination.

CSS is one of those powerful tools. In the previous chapter, we learned how to create a layout, control typography, and introduce interactivity to your Web designs. In this chapter, we're going to learn how to make your layouts beautiful.

Using Background Images

One of the easiest ways to create a visually interesting, on-brand page is to bring in graphics that were created in a program like Photoshop.

BRINGING IN DECORATIVE IMAGES WITH CSS

In previous chapters, I introduced you to the `<img>` tag in HTML. That tag is meant to bring in imagery that is considered content, like a headshot or a logo. In this chapter, we're going to be bringing in images with CSS, not HTML. So, if you want to bring in an image for decoration, like a repeating pattern in the background, or a grungy texture to serve as the base layer for your page, we'll do it with CSS using background images, not the `<img>` tag.

Rather than using the `<img>` tag with HTML to bring in a decorative image or pattern, we use the CSS property background-image in combination with a few other properties like background-repeat, background-color, and background-position:

```
.content{
   background-color: #DDD;
   background-image: url(i/tile.gif);
   background-repeat: repeat-x;
   background-position: right bottom;
   }
```

Why Define a Background Color?

You already know about the background-color property from the last chapter—plus it's pretty self-explanatory.

```
.content{
   background-color: #DDD;
   background-image: url(i/tile.gif);
   background-repeat: repeat-x;
   background-position: right bottom;
   }
```

A question I often get in my workshops is, "Why do I need to define a background color if it's going to be covered up by a big or repeating background image?"

It's really a great question because it brings up a good point about making the Web a friendlier place for everyone. As Web designers, we're designing for flexible content, different-sized screens, and users all over the globe with different preferences and download speeds. Therefore, we need to design for the worst-case scenario.

The worst-case scenario when we use images online is that the image doesn't load. This could happen for a number of reasons. Perhaps the Internet tubes are clogged and the image takes a long time to download. Or, perhaps your user is viewing your site from a place where Internet access is really slow, such as a third-world country or a lake cabin way out in the woods.

Before you go writing this off as an unlikely scenario, think of users who are in these areas to vacation, do mission work, or fight wars. It's more common than you might think.

For these users who have to wait a long time for the background image, or for whom the image doesn't load at all, we should define a background color to ensure that any text in that tag remains readable. A common scenario is when the designer puts white text on top of a dark background image. If the image doesn't load, or if it loads slowly, the white text will not be visible on the default white background color. To fix this, we set a dark background color to ensure the text is readable without images.

If you don't fix this, some of your users may not be able to read the text. I encourage you always to design for the worst-case scenario—being able to design something to be viewed in different ways by different users is what makes Web design so rewarding. And it's always appreciated by these users, who may not know how much effort went into the design, but who will remember that this Web site *just works*.

Specifying Paths for Background Images

In HTML, you learned how to use the src attribute to specify the path to an image. CSS has its own special way to call images, but paths work exactly the same way in CSS as they do in HTML:

```
.content{
  background-color: #DDD;
  background-image: url(i/tile.gif);
  background-repeat: repeat-x;
  background-position: right bottom;
  }
```

We're looking at two things here: the syntax we need to learn and the image path, which you'll remember from Chapter 3.

TIP When you look at someone else's pre-existing CSS you may notice them using tick marks in their path name, like this: url('i/tile.gif'). That's fine, but the marks aren't needed. I don't type them because they slow me down.

Let's start with the syntax. Instead of using the src attribute as in HTML, we write url(). The string url(with the opening parenthesis tells us we're about to set the path for an image. The closing parenthesis tells us we're done writing the image path:

url(i/tile.gif)

Now for the path. In Chapter 3, we learned how to write paths by navigating folders to locate the file. The path in the preceding example is a relative path (you can use absolute paths in CSS as well, but I recommend sticking with relative paths as a best practice) because it's relative to the location of the CSS file:

url(i/tile.gif)

In this example, I have named my CSS images folder i, which is an abbreviation I made up for images. Why did I do this? Two reasons. First, it's easier and faster to type i/ than it is to type images/. Second, this approach keeps the file size down—in a very large CSS file, if I write i/ instead of images/ there are fewer characters and the file size ends up being smaller.

In the preceding example, let's imagine we have the following folder structure:

- index.html (HTML file)
- css (folder)
  - base.css (CSS file)
  - i (folder)
    - tile.gif (image file)

Since the CSS file base.css is in the css folder, and the i folder is in the css folder, we just type i/tile.gif to get to tile.gif inside the css/i/ folder.

TIP The image path here needs to be relative to the CSS file (base.css) that's calling it, not the HTML file.

Repeating Background Images

You have been around the Internet long enough to know what a repeating background image looks like (**FIGURE 7.1**). There's no denying that this feature of CSS has been way overused.

But being the tasteful designer that you are, you wouldn't use this sort of image, would you?

All kidding aside, a repeating background image, when used right, can have a nice effect and add a layer of depth and texture to your design that makes it feel a lot more finished and professional.

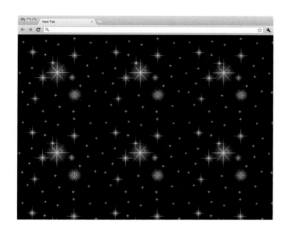

FIGURE 7.1
Background images are
nothing new as far as the
Internet is concerned.

Our example repeats the background image along the X-axis, but CSS gives
us other options.

```
.content{
  background-color: #DDD;
  background-image: url(i/tile.gif);
  background-repeat: repeat-x;
  background-position: right bottom;
  }
```

TABLE 7.1 lists the ways we can repeat a background image with the
background-repeat property.

TABLE 7.1   Values for background-repeat

CSS	ENGLISH
repeat	This tells the image to repeat up and down, left and right, in all directions.
no-repeat	This tells the image not to repeat. It's useful if you're using a single, larger image or if you are using a single image as a decoration, like a ghosted logo in the background.
repeat-x	This tells the image to repeat on the X-axis.
repeat-y	This tells the image to repeat on the, you guessed it, Y-axis.

FIGURE 7.2
I remember the Y-axis goes
up and down because of
the way the letter Y lines
up vertically on this graph.

And I know, I know. X- and Y-axis is hard to remember—so I came up with a
little graphic that helps me keep them straight (FIGURE 7.2).

Positioning Background Images

When you bring in a background image with CSS, the browser starts it at the left top corner of the tag you tell it to be in. For an image that's supposed to repeat in all directions, this is fine—it will repeat in every direction and fill up the container, regardless of the container's size.

But if you want your image to be placed in a specific place, or to repeat only in one direction or the other, you need to tell the browser where you want the image to start.

```
.content{
  background-color: #DDD;
  background-image: url(i/tile.gif);
  background-repeat: repeat-x;
  background-position: right bottom;
  }
```

The background-position property lets us use pixels, percentages, and keywords to control the starting point for our images.

Note that order matters with background-position. As you can see in our example, the background-position property accepts two values. The first value is the horizontal (left-right) position and the second value is the vertical (top-bottom) position.

Using Keywords for Position

TIP When you use keywords, your user's browser is smart enough to know what the keywords mean regardless of the order in which you write them. Just be careful when declaring center, because center horizontally and center vertically are two different things.

You can position a background image using plain English. Here's an example of what the code might look like:

```
.content{
  background-position: right bottom;
  }
```

Keywords are a nice feature of CSS that let us specify what we want in plain English. They're easy to write and easy to read. Top means top, bottom means bottom, left means left, right means right, and center means center (whether horizontal or vertical).

TABLE 7.2 lists our options for positioning a background image horizontally.

TABLE 7.2   Horizontal Positioning with Keywords

CSS	ENGLISH
left	This starts the image on the left side of the tag.
center	This centers the image horizontally.
right	This starts the image on the right side of the tag.

TABLE 7.3 lists our options for positioning a background image vertically.

TABLE 7.3   Vertical Positioning with Keywords

CSS	ENGLISH
top	This puts the image at the top of the tag.
center	This centers the image vertically.
bottom	This starts the image at the bottom of the tag.

Using Pixels for Position

You can precisely position a background image by counting in pixels from the left top corner of the tag specified. Here's an example of what your code might look like:

```
.content{
   background-position: 100px 200px;
   }
```

We already know that the first value is the horizontal position and the second value is the vertical position. So it's easy to see that this background image would be placed 100 pixels from the left and 200 pixels from the top of the tag specified (FIGURE 7.3).

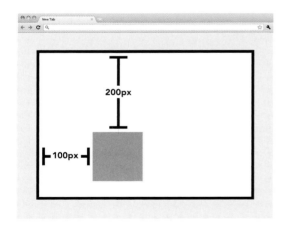

FIGURE 7.3
This background image has been positioned 100 pixels over from the left and 200 pixels down from the top.

TIP If you leave out a keyword, the browser assumes you meant to write center for the other axis. So typing background-position: right; is the same as typing background-position: right center; in your declaration. And typing background-position: bottom; is the same as typing background-position: center bottom; in your declaration.

CROPPING BACKGROUND IMAGES

You can use a negative pixel value to specify the position of a background image. Whatever "hangs out" of the specified tag will not show, similar to the way that in InDesign, after you import an image, you can crop out the parts that you don't want to use. *This cropping is something we'll make good use of later in this chapter, so be ready!*

Using Percentages for Position

Percentages provide a flexible way to position a background image relative to the top left of the tag specified. Here's an example of what the code might look like:

```
.content{
    background-position: 30% 70%;
    }
```

Positioning a background image with percentages can be fun, if a little confusing at first.

The simplest way to understand positioning with percentages is to calibrate our brains to the way percentages work in this context. If you position a background-image with 0% 0%, it's the same as starting in the left top corner. If you position a background image with 100% 100%, it's the same as starting at the right bottom corner. And 50% 50% is the same as centering the image horizontally and vertically.

You can use any value you want for the percentages and they will be positioned accordingly.

Using Shorthand for Background Images

I almost always use the shorthand background property for controlling anything that has to do with the background appearance. The shorthand looks like this.

```
background: #DDD url(i/tile.gif) repeat-x 10px 40px;
```

The shorthand saves a lot of time typing out long, redundant CSS properties. The background property accepts multiple values, each separated by a space.

• The first value is the background-color of the tag that's calling the background-image.

• The second value is the path to the background image.

- The third value tells whether or not the background image should repeat and, if so, in which direction.

- The fourth value positions the background image horizontally, from the left side of the tag.

- The fifth value positions the background image vertically, from the top of the tag.

Cropping Images with CSS

Earlier I mentioned that we'd learn how to make good use of our ability to crop images with CSS. Let's say you're laying out a poster with InDesign and you don't want to see part of an image—you just crop the image you've imported to get rid of the parts you don't want to see (FIGURE 7.4).

In the Web design world, we call these big images with parts cropped out *sprites*.

FIGURE 7.4 Cropping images with InDesign is a cinch.

Why Would You Do This?

You might wonder why we'd want to import an image and then display only part of it, because it means your users are downloading a file that's bigger than it needs to be. I'm glad you care so much about performance; you will do well as a Web designer.

But if you want to use the other part of that image later, this approach can come in handy.

In addition, each time the server requests a new image it slows the download speed. Downloading one large file is usually quicker than downloading gobs and gobs of tiny files, since each file is a hit on the server.

Creating Fancy Rollovers with Images

We create *sprites* by making an image in Photoshop (or whatever graphic-editing program you want to use) with multiple graphics on a larger canvas (FIGURE 7.5).

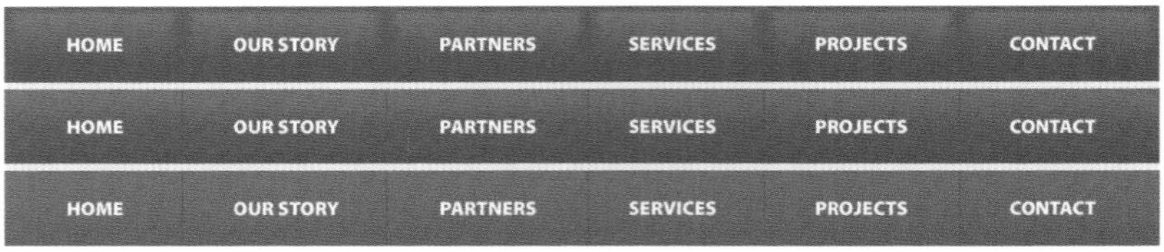

FIGURE 7.5 This is a sprite for a navigation menu. It shows a default state, rollover state, and pressed state.

Then we use the background-position property to crop the parts of the graphic that we don't want to see (FIGURE 7.6).

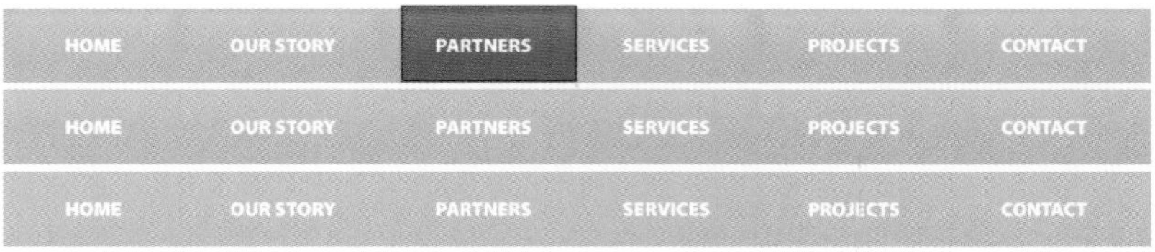

FIGURE 7.6
By positioning the background image, we're able to show selective parts of a sprite. Here we're showing a pressed state for the Partners menu item.

Let's say you want to design a download button that's monochromatic in its default state, but changes to orange when you hover over it. You would use the :hover pseudo-selector we learned about in Chapter 6 to change the background-position to reveal the color version of the icon and hide the monochromatic version.

Let me say that without the technical words: To create rollovers with CSS, all you need to do is change the position of an image when you roll over it to show the rollover state and hide the default state. Let's do it.

For this example, let's make a simple download link for a resume
(FIGURE 7.7).

FIGURE 7.7
The default state on the
left changes to orange
when a user rolls over the
links with her mouse.

1. Write the HTML and create the image (FIGURE 7.8).

```
<div class="download">
  <a href="downloads/resume.pdf">Download</a>
</div>
```

2. Use what you learned above to bring in the background image
   (FIGURE 7.9).

FIGURE 7.9
Before you style the link,
the text overlays the
background image.

```
.download a{
  background: url(icon-download.gif) no-repeat right top;
}
```

Notice how we left out the values for background-color. Doing this
makes it transparent. So what we wrote is the same as if we had
written this:

```
.download a{
  background: transparent url(icon-download.gif) no-repeat right top;
}
```

3. Notice how part of the download icon is sitting behind the link. This is
   no good, so add some padding to the right side of the download link
   to make room for the icon to be visible. Also add some padding all
   the way around the link, and style the text so it starts to look more like
   what we want (FIGURE 7.10).

FIGURE 7.10
With some padding and
text treatments, this looks
like a nice link.

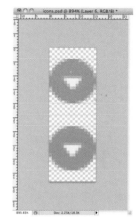

FIGURE 7.8 A small
sprite with the gray and
orange graphics for the
rollover effect.

```
.download a{
    background: url(icon-download.gif) no-repeat right top;
    padding: 5px 20px 5px 5px;
    font-size: 12px;
    font-family: "Helvitica Neue", helvetica, arial, sans-serif;
    text-decoration: none;
    color: #444; /* dark gray text color */
}
```

TIP I make it my personal goal to write as little CSS as possible. You should, too!

4. The bottom part of the graphic we brought in is not visible because it's hanging outside beyond the edges of the tag. Let's switch out the graphic on :hover to reveal the rollover state of the graphic and make the default state hang outside of the tag (FIGURE 7.11). While we're at it, let's also give the link text a matching orange color on :hover.

FIGURE 7.11 On the left, the orange graphic is hidden. When a user rolls over the link, the background position changes to reveal the orange graphic and hide the gray one.

TIP Overriding CSS declarations downstream like this is a common practice and is part of what gives CSS its power. We'll learn more about this in Chapter 9.

Since the only characteristic of the background image we're changing is the background position, we don't need to use the shorthand to specify everything again. We'll just use the background-position property to override that one part of our previous statement.

```
.download a{
    background: url(icon-download.gif) no-repeat right top;
    padding: 5px 20px 5px 5px;
    font-size: 12px;
    font-family: "Helvitica Neue", helvetica, arial, sans-serif;
    text-decoration: none;
    color: #444; /* dark gray text color */
}

.download a:hover{
    background-position: right bottom;
    color: #E56121;
}
```

Creating Image-Based Rollovers

Now that you've seen how to swap out an image when you roll over a link, let's take it a step further. Let's say you wanted to create a big honkin' "Buy Now" button that looks so delicious your users can't help but click it (FIGURE 7.12).

FIGURE 7.12 It's hard not to click this big green monster.

This button has a special typeface, subtle gradients, depth, and texture. It's easy to create in Photoshop—you can do things like this in your sleep. But to turn this into an interactive button with :hover and :active states will take some serious CSS skills. Or will it?

All we have to do is use what we've learned, plus one little trick. Rather than trying to style the text to match what we've designed, let's make the entire link a CSS background image.

Start by writing the HTML and creating a sprite (FIGURE 7.13). We can use some familiar HTML from our last example.

FIGURE 7.13 This sprite has a default state (top), a rollover state (center), and a pressed state (bottom).

```
<div class="buy">
  <a href="add-to-cart.php">Buy Now</a>
</div>
```

With CSS, bring in the background image.

```
.buy a{
  background: green url(buy-now.gif) no-repeat top;
}
```

Next, we want to make the <a> tag the same size as the button graphic. The sprite is 200 pixels wide and 225 pixels tall, but that's because it contains all three states for the button. We'll make the link 200 pixels wide by 75 pixels tall and hide the other states in the sprite for now.

An <a> tag is an inline tag by default, so if we want to specify a width and height we need to tell it to display: block; before the width and height will work.

```
.buy a{
  background: green url(buy-now.gif) no-repeat top;
  display: block;
  width: 200px;
  height: 75px;
}
```

Uh-oh, the text is overlaying the background image. This happened in our earlier example for a moment before we added padding to make room for the icon. In this example, we don't want the text to show at all. There's a simple fix for this called *image replacement*.

Image replacement is a Web designer's way of getting rid of the text with CSS, while keeping it in the HTML. This way, the HTML can still be read when viewed on a browser that doesn't support CSS, in an RSS reader, and by Google.

Here's one common way to use image replacement:

```
.buy a{
  background: green url(buy-now.gif) no-repeat top;
  display: block;
  width: 200px;
  height: 75px;
  text-indent: -9999px;
}
```

Look at that closely. We're using a new property called text-indent and we're setting its value to an obscenely high negative pixel value. This technique takes the text inside of the tag you target and throws it way out to the left so it won't be seen (FIGURE 7.14).

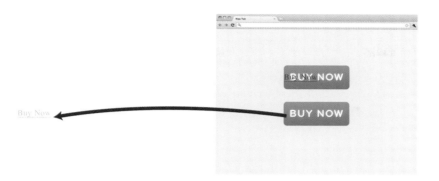

FIGURE 7.14 Image replacement takes the text and literally throws it way off the Web page so it's out of the way of the background image.

The words "Buy Now" are still in the HTML, but the CSS has effectively hidden them and replaced them with an image.

Finally, let's add some CSS to control the rollover and pressed states.

```
.buy a{
   background: green url(buy-now.gif) no-repeat top;
   display: block;
   width: 200px;
   height: 75px;
   text-indent: -9999px;
}

.download a:hover{
   background-position: center;
   }

.download a:active{
   background-position: bottom;
   }
```

A Word of Caution About Image Replacement

We learned earlier why it's always important to set a background-color value so text remains readable when a user's images don't load. Well, image replacement isn't perfect.

The worst-case scenario here is that the image doesn't load and the text is negative indented so that it's not visible. This means a user whose images don't load will not be able to see the link. Always be thinking about these things when designing Web sites—identify the people who will be using your Web site and design for them.

TIP There are other techniques out there that are much more advanced than this with their own pros and cons. I've created a page at cssforprintdesigners. com/image-replacement where you can learn more.

Use Your Imagination

When it comes to using background images with CSS, you're limited only by your imagination. As I've said before, I'm only giving you the tips and tricks that get me through the majority of my workday as a Web designer. Get creative, practice these techniques, try new things, and see what works.

Making Columns with Background Images

There's one last concept we need to cover before we move past CSS images: columns. I know what you're thinking—we covered floats for columns in the last chapter. Well, I left something out, conveniently, until now.

CSS doesn't give us a good way to make columns that stretch all the way down the page, because tags stretch vertically only as far as they need to. So if you have a columnar layout, one column may be longer than the other (**FIGURE 7.15**). That's because CSS and HTML were created to let content flow as long or as short as it needs.

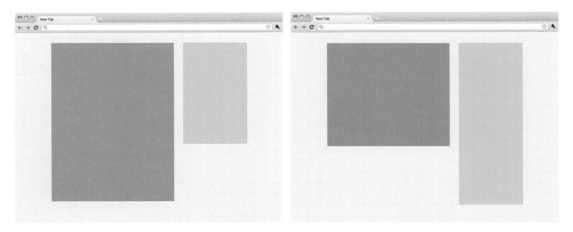

FIGURE 7.15 On the Web, vertical height is determined by how much content is inside a tag.

Tags grow vertically to let the content flow and then stop when the content ends. There's no way with CSS to tell both of these columns to be the same height. They are independent of one another and grow based only on the content that fills them.

YOU CAN SET A MINIMUM HEIGHT THOUGH

CSS gives us the min-height property, which helps, but doesn't solve our problem once the content grows beyond the minimum height. The min-height property is like the height property in that it sets the height of a tag. The difference is that with min-height, we're allowing the area to expand if content grows longer than the space allotted.

Give Up on Vertical Alignment Already

As print designers, we like things to line up. And it makes sense, because we're used to designing for a space that is usually rectangular with a defined width and height.

As you transition from a print designer into a Web designer, I want you to come to terms with the fact that vertical alignment in Web design is nearly impossible. There are too many factors with dynamic content and user settings to control it.

Plus, the Web is optimized for reading top to bottom—it doesn't have a fixed height like a magazine or newspaper or brochure. It's more like a scroll that unrolls to be as long as it needs to be. Web pages, like these old-timey scrolls, are optimized to grow in length to accommodate any amount of content—hence the term *scroll bar*.

This lack of fixed dimensions is often frustrating for print designers because it makes it difficult for us to line things up vertically.

Don't get down on Web design just yet. In a way, it's liberating—we don't have a fixed height! We can make the page as long as we want.

Making Fake Columns

In 2004, Dan Cederholm published an article in *A List Apart, No. 167* entitled "Faux Columns" where he describes a simple concept for faking the vertical alignment of columns. He didn't invent the technique, but his article was the first time I encountered the trick, and it blew my mind.

In short, you create a background image in Photoshop and position it to repeat on the Y-axis behind the columns, which creates the illusion of a column that always matches the height of its sibling columns.

It's a hack, but it's a simple hack, and it works.

To do this, you put a background image inside the parent container for the columns and repeat it vertically so it stretches the entire height of the longest column.

Here's a sample image you might use; let's call it column.gif (FIGURE 7.16). This image matches the width of the column and defines the space with a subtle gradient to give a sense of depth.

FIGURE 7.16 If we repeat this background image behind a column, we can make that column look like it's aligned vertically with other columns.

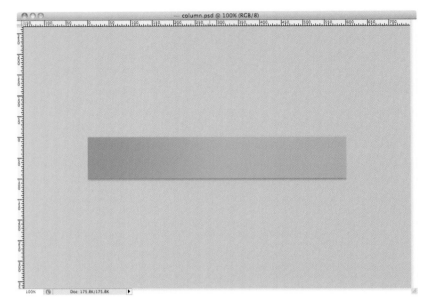

Now let's write some HTML, which should look familiar to you by now.

```
<div class="content">
  <div class="main">
    <p>
      We will put a lot of content in here. That is because we want this
      ⇒ column to be much taller than the side column. As this column
      ⇒ grows in size, we want the side column to appear to grow with
      ⇒ it. We are faking this by repeating a background-image on the
      ⇒ parent container.
    </p>
    <p>
      This paragraph is just here for good measure. Are you really
      ⇒ reading this?
    </p>
  </div>
  <div class="side">
```

```
<p>
   We will put just a little bit of content in here.
</p>
</div>
</div>
```

And we'll write some CSS to create our columns.

```
.content{
  overflow: hidden;
  width: 960px;
  }

  .main{
    width: 720px;
    float: left;
    }

  .side{
    width: 200px;
    float: right;
    }
```

Finally, we'll add the magic CSS.

```
.content{
  overflow: hidden;
  width: 960px;
  background: #FFF url(i/column.gif) repeat-y right;
  }

  .main{
    width: 760px;
    float: left;
    }

  .side{
    width: 200px;
    float: right;
    }
```

Now that we've placed the background image you can see how it will grow vertically to fill the space regardless of the height of the content (FIGURE 7.17). It's a simple trick, but it helps Web designers every day.

FIGURE 7.17 This Web page makes you think the column heights are aligned, but they're not. We're just faking it with a repeating background image.

Designing with CSS3—Without Images

It's a fact: Designers love things like rounded corners and drop shadows. Who can blame us? They're pretty! And until recently, we had to rely on creative uses of background images to accomplish these things. Now, though, we have better browsers (like Firefox, Safari, Chrome, and Internet Explorer 9) that let us use newer techniques for getting our rounded-corner fix.

I told you in Chapter 5 how HTML5 is the new version of HTML, and that it's basically adding a few things on top of the old HTML to make it better. Well, CSS3 is the same way—all the stuff we've learned so far has been part of CSS for some time, but CSS3 is giving us some new ways to do some cool things like add rounded corners and drop shadows without using images.

TIP CSS3 also gives us ways to create simple animations without using JavaScript. But that's some pretty advanced stuff, so I'm leaving it out of this book. You can see some demos of CSS animations at cssforprintdesigners.com/css-animations.

Pros and Cons of CSS3

While there are definitely benefits to using images for decoration (such as wider browser support), relying on images also has some negative side effects (such as added load times and production costs for businesses).

You're just now learning to code Web sites, so I'm going to teach you the new way—I don't think there's much point in teaching you the old way to do things if it's going to be replaced by something better very soon. As each day passes, more users are using browsers that support these CSS3 techniques, so I say go for it.

Before we know it, this won't even be a discussion. But for now, we have to know the implications of using the latest and greatest.

The biggest concern with using CSS3 is browser support. I still have this discussion with clients on almost every project: Does it need to look exactly the same in all browsers? Usually, the immediate response is, "What's a browser?" Then, after an explanation, the answer is, "Yes, of course the content in all browsers should match."

Graceful Degradation

This is a great time to introduce a Web design concept to your client called *graceful degradation*. Graceful degradation is a fancy way of saying that a Web design looks (or behaves, in some instances) a little different in older browsers because it's built for future compatibility. Overall, the layout and functionality will stay the same—but little things like rounded corners or drop shadows will not make it to the older browsers.

The Web site won't look *broken* to those users, and they'll never know it's different since they're not going to be looking at the site side by side in different browsers checking to see if the rounded corners match.

If you can sell this idea to your clients, you're at a point where you can start using CSS3 to save yourself a lot of time in developing workarounds with background images for common elements like rounded corners and drop shadows.

Selling Clients on CSS3

Here's the ideal conversation I would have with my clients.

Me: "For your project, we can save you some money by using CSS3 for some of the design treatments like rounded corners and drop shadows. Your Web site will also load faster for everybody. It's a best practice."

Client: "Fantastic, I *love* best practices. Why are you telling me this?"

Me: "You need to know that some of your users on older computers won't see the design the exact same way; they'll get square corners instead, and they won't see the shadows. But overall, the design will still look good. Are you okay with that?"

Client: "Did you say it would save me money?"

Me: "Yes."

Client: "Why are you still standing here? Get to work!"

TIP Another approach is just to do it without telling them. I haven't gotten any complaints (yet) when I've done that.

But let's be honest—sometimes the client will insist that the site look exactly the same in all browsers. Something about *branding*. What do you want me to say? You can't win 'em all.

The Ugly Truth About CSS3 (For Now)

Remember how I told you CSS3 is new? Yeah, well, it's not even finished yet.

I'm oversimplifying the problem here, but I doubt you read all the gossip magazines for Web design, so I'll leave it oversimplified. The exciting CSS3 properties that create things like rounded corners and drop shadows are not finalized yet, so browser makers have created their own CSS3 properties in the meantime.

This means that what makes a corner round in Firefox doesn't necessarily make it round in Safari and Chrome, so for now we've got to write CSS multiple times to make sure each browser gets the rounded corner. Thankfully, the new Internet Explorer 9 does a pretty good job with CSS3.

Still, in my opinion, you need to be learning CSS3 because it's easier than creating images for these simple design treatments, and it loads faster—plus it's the future, not the past.

That is, of course, assuming your client is OK with older browsers not having all the CSS3 awesomeness.

Browser Wars

To understand this issue fully, we need to go off on a slight tangent and talk about browsers and how browsers are made. Different companies make different browsers; to be competitive with each other they think it's smart to use different *rendering engines* to display Web pages.

The rendering engine determines the way the browser interprets HTML and CSS and decides what to display when you visit a Web site.

Since the makers of browsers don't all use the same rendering engine, Web designers sometimes need to learn different ways to accomplish the same thing in different browsers. Add on top of this that each browser has rendering bugs and you can see how troubleshooting CSS can become a headache.

Don't worry; for the most part, modern browsers are starting to agree on how things should render. But with something as new as CSS3, there are bound to be differences.

BROWSER-SPECIFIC PREFIXES

Firefox uses its own rendering engine, so its CSS3 properties are pre-fixed with -moz-, which is short for Mozilla, the organization that makes Firefox. Safari and Chrome both use the same rendering engine called Webkit, so their CSS3 properties are prefixed with -webkit-. Other browser makers have different rendering engines as well. Learn more at cssforprintdesigners.com/browsers.

The Best Way Forward with CSS3

Browser makers have thankfully been very deliberate about prefixed CSS properties. Safari and Chrome will ignore any CSS declaration that begins with -moz-, Firefox will ignore any declaration that begins with -webkit-, and so on. This makes it possible for us to write CSS that works well on one browser without causing problems in another browser.

My recommendation is to write your CSS so that it's as future-proof as possible. To do this, we'll write the vendor-specific CSS properties first, and then end with the proposed CSS3 property. Here's a quick example of how I'd recommend making rounded corners on a tag with CSS3.

```
.container{
  -moz-border-radius: 10px;
  -webkit-border-radius: 10px;
  border-radius: 10px;
}
```

We've written basically the same thing three times, with the only difference being the vendor-specific prefix. Ideally, you'll be able to come back to your code in a few years and remove the vendor-specific prefixes to clean up your code, but these prefixes are designed in a way that it doesn't hurt anything to leave them in there—especially if your last CSS declaration is the CSS3 standard without a prefix. That's because if there's ever a conflict, your browser will use the last CSS declaration to override previous declarations.

> **TIP** CSS3 support is changing so much that your best resource is the Internet. I've made a page at cssforprintdesigners.com/css3 where you can keep up with the latest browser support and techniques for CSS3.

> **TIP** There's more to learn about this thing called overriding in Chapter 9.

Using Rounded Corners

Every designer knows rounded corners make things prettier; that's just the way it is. We achieve rounded corners with CSS3 using the border-radius property.

```
.container{
  border-radius: 10px;
}
```

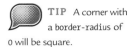

TIP A corner with a border-radius of 0 will be square.

Just as with the padding and margin properties, we can declare all four corners at once, or we can declare them individually, clockwise. To do this, we start with the top-left corner and work our way around the tag clockwise.

```
.container{
    border-radius: 10px 20px 30px 40px;
}
```

In a perfect world, we'd be done. But since we want to make sure as many browsers as possible see the rounded corners, let's layer on some vendor-specific prefixes, just to be safe.

```
.container{
    -moz-border-radius-topleft: 10px;
    -moz-border-radius-topright: 20px;
    -moz-border-radius-bottomright: 30px;
    -moz-border-radius-bottomleft: 40px;
    -webkit-border-top-left-radius: 10px;
    -webkit-border-top-right-radius: 20px;
    -webkit-border-bottom-right-radius: 30px;
    -webkit-border-bottom-left-radius: 40px;
    border-radius: 10px 20px 30px 40px;
}
```

TIP I have a list of my favorite CSS3 generators over at the same link I mentioned earlier: cssforprintdesigners.com/css3.

Notice how Mozilla and Webkit browsers slightly differ in their syntax, in addition to the vendor-specific prefix.

Yuck. OK, seriously. I don't even try and memorize this stuff. There are great CSS3 generators online that will help you generate this gobbledygook without straining your brain.

Adding Shadows

Designers love depth. And clients love things that pop. We can add depth and pop to our designs with drop-shadows. CSS3 lets us create shadows for a box with the box-shadow property and shadows for text with the text-shadow property.

Putting Shadows on Boxes

Using the box-shadow property with CSS3 is similar to using the drop-shadow layer effect in Photoshop (FIGURE 7.18).

The property accepts several values to make it work (FIGURE 7.19).

```
.container{
    box-shadow: 5px -5px 8px 2px #888;
}
```

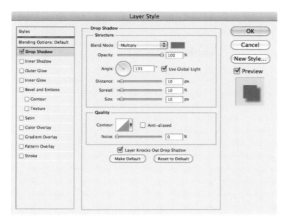

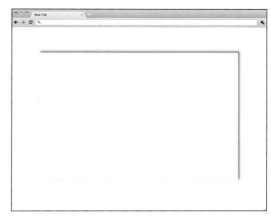

FIGURE 7.18 Controlling shadows with CSS3 is a lot like using the drop-shadow layer effect in Photoshop.

FIGURE 7.19 A CSS3 box-shadow.

- The first value moves the shadow left or right. If you use a negative value like -5px, it moves the shadow to the left. A positive value like 5px moves it to the right.

- The second value moves the shadow up or down. If you use a negative value like -5px, it moves the shadow up. A positive value like 5px moves the shadow down.

- The third value controls the blur size of the shadow, which is sort of like the size of the shadow in Photoshop's drop-shadow settings.

- The fourth value is the spread size of the shadow. I usually just play with this until it looks right.

- The fifth value is the color of the shadow. If you want it to be more opaque, choose a darker color; if you want it to be less opaque, choose a lighter color.

A REAL TRANSPARENT SHADOW

If you want real transparency, you can use an RGBa value in place of a hexadecimal value. RGBa is the same as RGB, which I mentioned earlier in the book, but it adds an alpha transparency value to the end, which controls transparency. A gray shadow at 50% opacity would be written like this: rgba(0,0,0,0.5). But be careful; older browsers don't support RGBa colors.

In addition, you can add the inset keyword at the beginning of your values to make the shadow an inner shadow, as in Photoshop (FIGURE 7.20). You'd do it like this:

FIGURE 7.20 A CSS3 box-shadow with the inset keyword applied.

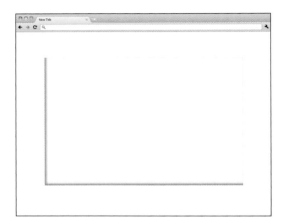

```
.container{
    box-shadow: inset 5px -5px 2px 8px #888;
    }
```

Now, to make sure most browsers will render your beautiful drop shadow, we need to write our final CSS like this, with vendor-specific prefixes:

```
.container{
    -moz-box-shadow: inset 5px -5px 2px 8px #888;
    -webkit-box-shadow: inset 5px -5px 2px 8px #888;
    box-shadow: inset 5px -5px 2px 8px #888;
    }
```

Just as when you're designing for print, it's best to play with these values to get the best results. And don't worry; I find myself looking up which value does what every time I make a drop shadow with CSS3. That is, if I'm not being lazy—most of the time I just start nudging the values up and down to see which direction the shadow goes and how it looks.

Putting Shadows on Text

With CSS3 we can use the text-shadow property to put a drop shadow on text (FIGURE 7.21). As if making your boxes pop wasn't enough, now there's no excuse for not having enough pop in your design.

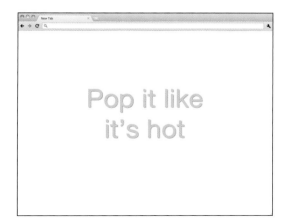

FIGURE 7.21 A CSS3 text-shadow.

We use the text-shadow property in much the same way that we use the box-shadow property:

```
h1{
   text-shadow: 2px 2px 2px #888;
   }
```

- The first value moves the shadow left or right. If you use a negative value like -2px, it moves the shadow to the left. A positive value like 2px moves it to the right.

- The second value moves the shadow up or down. If you use a negative value like -2px, it moves the shadow up. A positive value like 2px moves the shadow down.

- The third value controls the blur size of the shadow, which is sort of like the size of the shadow in Photoshop's drop-shadow settings.

- The fourth value is the color of the shadow. If you want it to be more opaque, choose a darker color; if you want it to be less opaque, choose a lighter color.

Putting It All Together

Let's walk through a simple Web page design using background images and CSS3 to see what we can make (FIGURE 7.22).

First, we'll need to create a sprite for the big button (FIGURE 7.23).

FIGURE 7.22 With just what you've learned in this chapter, you have the tools you need to start making attractive Web sites.

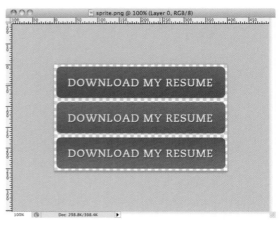

FIGURE 7.23 A sprite that contains a default state, rollover state, and pressed state for the download button.

Second, we write the HTML.

```
<div class="container">
  <header>
    <h1>My name is JD.</h1>
  </header>
  <div id="content">
    <p class="intro">
      I am a Web designer from Memphis, and I run a Web design firm
      ➥called <a href="http://simplefocus.com/">Simple Focus</a>. I am
      ➥also on the board for <a href="http://memphis.aiga.org/">
      ➥AIGA Memphis</a>. In my spare time I like to fish and write
      ➥poetry.
    </p>
    <div class="download">
      <a href="downloads/resume.pdf">Download My Resume</a>
    </div>
  </div>
</div><!-- close .container -->
```

Finally, we add the CSS.

```
.container{
  width: 400px;
  padding: 40px; /* The total width is 480px! */
  margin: 100px auto; /* put space above and below, then center the tag
  ➥in the browser */
```

```
background-color: orange;
-moz-border-radius: 20px; /* rounded corners for Mozilla */
-webkit-border-radius: 20px; /* rounded corners for Webkit */
border-radius: 20px; /* CSS3 rounded corners for new browsers */
-moz-box-shadow: 0 3px 5px 0 #AAA; /* for Mozilla */
-webkit-box-shadow: 0 3px 5px 0 #AAA; /* for Webkit */
box-shadow: 0 3px 5px 0 #AAA; /* CSS3 box-shadow for new browsers */
-moz-text-shadow: 1px 1px 1px #666; /* for Mozilla */
-webkit-text-shadow: 1px 1px 1px #666; /* for Webkit */
text-shadow: 1px 1px 1px #666; /* CSS3 text-shadow for new browsers */
font-family: "Helvetica Neue", helvetica, arial, sans-serif; /* since
➥ we are putting this on the parent tag, it applies to all the children
➥ as well */
color: #FFF; /* applies to all children */
text-align: center; /* applies to all children */
}

a{
   color: #FFF; /* changing the default blue color */
   }

a:hover{
   text-decoration: none; /* rollover */
   }

a:active{
   color: gold; /* pressed */
   }

h1{
   margin: 0; /* removing unnecessary default spacing for headings */
   font-size: 36px; /* make it bigger */
   font-weight: normal; /* lose the default bold */
   padding-bottom: 20px; /* add some space below */
   }

p{
   margin: 0; /* removing unnecessary default spacing for paragraphs */
   font-size: 18px; /* make it bigger */
   }

.download a{
```

TIP You can see this Web page in action at cssforprintdesigners.com/mysite.

```
background: url(i/sprite.png) no-repeat top; /* bring in the sprite
➥ image */
display: block; /* changing its appearance from default inline to
➥ block */
width: 400px; /* this width happens to match the width set for
➥ .container */
height: 85px; /* the height of one of the graphics in the sprite,
➥ inlcuding shadows */
text-indent: -9999px; /* get rid of the overlapping text */
margin-top: 20px; /* add some space above the button */
}

.download a:hover{
background-position: center; /* rollover */
}

.download a:active{
background-position: bottom; /* pressed */
}
```

Making Design Happen

So far I have given you the most powerful, reusable, and common prop-erties and techniques for CSS. But I'm not going to pretend I've even scratched the surface of CSS in this chapter (or in this book, for that mat-ter). Truth is, I've left out hundreds of CSS properties, values, and tech-niques that wield enormous power.

As with the rest of this book, my goal has been to lay down enough knowl-edge to empower you to take CSS head-on. With what you know now, you can accomplish almost anything you want—and Google for the rest.

Think of CSS as just another creative tool like InDesign, Photoshop, or even just pencil and paper. It's nothing more than a means for accomplishing your creative vision. Your creativity, outside of the tools you use, is what makes design happen.

8

Improving Lives with CSS

Making the Web a Friendlier Place

I LOVE CREATIVE people because they're typically some of the friendliest people I know. I'm talking about print designers, Web designers, toy designers, interior designers, illustrators, type designers, architects, photographers, writers, and fine artists (I can just as easily be talking about CPAs, doctors, lawyers, and anyone else who applies creative thinking in their work).

But the creative industry, especially, is full of nice people. People who may seem complicated, dark, or broody at first: Tattoos, weird music, and lack of overhead lighting are clear signs you're in the creative department.

Creative people have a special ability to use their imaginations to put themselves in someone else's shoes and to visualize what could be. They have the empathy required to feel someone else's frustration with a poor design, and then visualize a way to fix it.

And empathy is what we're going to cover in this chapter.

Empathy Through CSS

There are some things we should take into consideration when designing and coding Web sites that may seem unnecessary or optional at first, but they make the Web a friendlier place for all of our users.

These things may not be apparent early in the design process when you're sketching ideas on a whiteboard or laying out your Web page in Photoshop. But rest assured, they add up to make your Web page more useful (and less frustrating) to more people.

Things like

- How can we control what a Web page looks like when it's printed?

- How can we code and design Web sites that are usable by everyone, including blind, deaf, and mobility-impaired users?

- How can we write CSS so our Web sites load fast and perform well?

We're not going to go into great detail on how to accomplish all of these things in this chapter. But that's not because it's not important—it's because you already know most of what you need to know from the previous chapters.

Designing for Print (with CSS)

You heard it right; we're about to learn how to design for print with CSS! That's because your visitors will eventually print out a Web page from your site.

For me, there's just something about holding the written word in my hands—I don't know if it's usability or nostalgia. I can take it with me, scratch on it with my favorite pen, and read it on the plane, during a taxi ride, or in bed with my wonderful wife and spoiled beagle. Paper is real, so it makes the words feel more real. And finally, it's easier on the eyes than a backlit screen.

Since we design Web sites to work on screens that don't have a fixed vertical height, we have to think about what we want our Web sites to look like when they're printed out on letter-sized paper (FIGURE 8.1).

Writing Print Style Sheets

When you write your HTML, you have the ability to link to a separate CSS file that controls what your Web site looks like when it is printed. To hook to a CSS file, we use the `<link>` tag with attributes like rel, href, type, and media. The media attribute tells the browser to use this particular file when printing the page.

FIGURE 8.1 A print style sheet can be nicely designed, but it needs to be all business. Don't waste your users' ink because you want them to see that textured background.

We'll learn about linking to CSS files in Chapter 9, "Starting from Scratch," but here's a quick preview:

```
<link rel="stylesheet" href="css/print.css" type="text/css" media="print" />
```

What's great is you don't have to change your HTML to make a printer-friendly style sheet. All you have to do is write a separate CSS file.

Let's go through some of the things you may want to change about your site's appearance with a print style sheet.

Typography

Be sure to think about typography when you create a print style sheet. Odds are your user is printing the page to read it, so you should make a point to design for readability.

Font Size

You will remember in the Chapter 6 section "Selecting Units of Measurement" that we discussed a few different units of measurement. Pixels work great for the screen, but I suggest using points when making a print style sheet. The abbreviation is pt.

Here's an example:

```
p{
  font-size: 10pt;
  }
```

Color

For readability (and to save ink) I recommend turning all of your type dark and putting it on a white background.

Width

It's a good idea to get rid of any fixed widths for your content, so it can grow horizontally to fill the page, using as little paper as possible.

Printer Ink Is Not Cheap

There's nothing more frustrating to me than when I click Print on a Web page and walk over to the printer to realize I just printed seven pages of solid ink with white text on it that's barely readable.

A printed Web page should not waste ink by

- Printing unnecessary colors
- Printing reversed text (like white text on a black background)
- Showing sidebars or modules that don't make sense in a printed context (like navigation or sign-in forms)

To test your print style sheet without wasting ink and paper, you can just print a PDF of the page (FIGURE 8.2).

TIP You can learn more about print style sheets at cssfor-printdesigners.com/printer-friendly.

FIGURE 8.2 Rather than testing a print style sheet by actually printing the page, you can test it by printing a PDF file.

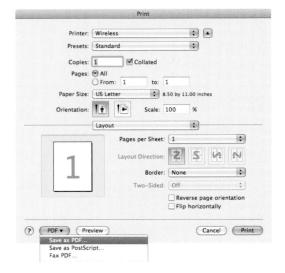

Designing for Accessibility

Everybody should have access to information on the Internet, regardless of ability or disability. As you design Web sites, don't forget that there are different ways that people access the information online than with their hands, eyes, and ears.

Vision Impairments

Not everyone who gets online can see your design, so you need to account for these visitors by designing *accessible* Web sites. "But wait," you ask, "How can I design for someone who can't see?"

Some People Can See, Just Not Well

A lot of people online have eyesight that's not very good, especially now that the plus-50 crowd is online—computers and the Internet are not just for young people any more. Be sure to design type that's readable by being big enough with plenty of contrast.

Blind Users Get Online, Too

Braille gives blind people the ability to read the written word. For reading online, there's software called *screen readers* that reads content aloud to people who are unable to see it.

Using HTML Attributes for Accessibility

You're already familiar with the alt attribute in the <img> tag, which describes the content of the image in case the image doesn't load. It's also what's read to a blind user by screen reading software.

There's another attribute we haven't discussed previously for <a> tags called title. The title attribute is like the alt attribute in that it tells a little more about the link, specifically where it's going to take the user when she clicks it. It's useful when the link text doesn't do a good job of describing its destination. An example of this is the overused "Click here," which doesn't tell the user where she's going.

Hearing Impairments

Captioning on television helps ensure that deaf people can watch television and know what's being said.

If your Web site has video or audio content, you can make captioning available to deaf users by providing alternate access to that content.

Making Captions and Transcripts Available

It doesn't take any CSS tricks to make captions available. You just embed subtitles into a video or provide a link to a transcript of an audio or video clip nearby where the media controls are located.

Mobility Impairments

Some users of the Internet have physical limitations that prevent them from being able to use a mouse effectively or at all.

Designing for Easy Targets

Since some users might have difficulty using a mouse, we should design links, buttons, and other *hit areas* in our designs so that they're big enough that clicking something isn't a challenge. About 30 pixels or more in size is a good start if you're making hit areas that are easy to click. The bigger the better.

Designing for Users Who Don't Use a Mouse

Some users of the Internet are unable to use a mouse. They navigate the Internet by giving commands some other way—usually through some sort of input device that accepts a command to tab to the next clickable item on the page.

In fact, this is a lot like using the Tab key on your own keyboard to navigate a Web site. Using the Tab key is actually a really good way to test your Web site's accessibility.

When you're testing your Web site for accessibility using the Tab key to navigate, it should be apparent at all times where you are on the page. You've seen this location information before on Web sites when there's a dotted outline around a link you've focused on.

If you can navigate your Web site using only the Tab and Return keys on your keyboard, your Web site is probably pretty accessible.

Using CSS to Show You Where You Are

Previously we learned about the :hover and :active pseudo-selectors for making Web pages more interactive. There's another pseudo-selector called :focus that lets you define what something should look like when a user has tabbed onto it with the keyboard instead of rolling over it with the mouse (FIGURE 8.3).

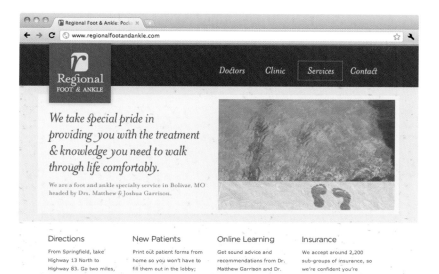

FIGURE 8.3 The dotted outline shows where you are when navigating this Web page without a mouse.

Here's some sample CSS that helps accessibility:

```
a:focus{
   outline: 1px dotted;
   }
```

Notice we're using the outline property, not border. The difference between the outline property and the border property is that outline is drawn on the outside of the border.

Writing CSS That Loads Fast

One last point to consider when you're trying to make a Web site that's pleasant to use is how fast it loads. The download speed can be affected by a number of things beyond your control such as server speed and the Internet connection.

I want to equip you for those things you can control.

Keep Your Images as Small as Possible

As you start using background images with CSS, don't go overboard. Think of creative ways to accomplish your design treatment with a smaller background image.

TIP I'll go into detail on exporting images for the Web in Chapter 10.

When saving your images, always use the best format for the type of image it is (FIGURE 8.4).

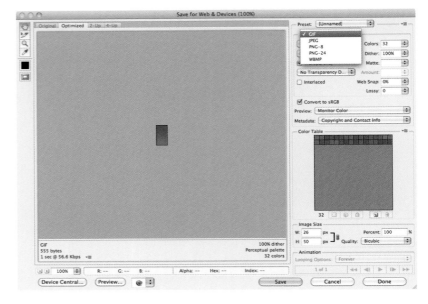

Remember, the smaller your images are, the faster the page will load. Plus, optimizing your images will make the biggest difference in page speed by far. If you don't do this, the rest won't matter.

Write Your CSS as Efficiently as Possible

Take the time to think ahead and plan your CSS before you start writing it. Writing your CSS to make it as compact as possible doesn't just save on file size and download speeds, it also saves you from a lot of unnecessary typing.

Stringing Together Selectors

One of the best ways to make your CSS more efficient is to string together selectors into a single CSS rule. It's a good idea to do this when several tags on your page need the same properties, like the header, content, and footer areas.

Consider this CSS, which isn't very efficient because it repeats the same declarations for each CSS rule:

```
header{
  width: 960px;
  margin: auto;
  overflow: hidden;
}
```

```
#content{
  width: 960px;
  margin: auto;
  overflow: hidden;
  }

footer{
  width: 960px;
  margin: auto;
  overflow: hidden;
  }
```

By stringing together our selectors with commas, we can write the same thing with a lot fewer keystrokes, saving time and file size.

```
header, #content, footer{
  width: 960px;
  margin: auto;
  overflow: hidden;
  }
```

You can put each selector on one line as in the preceding example, or you can put the selectors on separate lines with commas, like this:

```
header,
#content,
footer{
  width: 960px;
  margin: auto;
  overflow: hidden;
  }
```

Using Greater Specificity to Override Other CSS

You can override one CSS declaration with another by being more specific with the selector.

To see what I mean, take a look at this HTML:

```
<div id="content">
  <p class="teaser">What color am I?</p>
</div>
```

Let's say I wanted to make every paragraph in my design black. I might write my CSS like this:

```
p{
  color: black;
  }
```

But let's say I also wanted every paragraph with a class attribute of teaser to be purple. I'd write my CSS like this:

```
p{
  color: black;
  }

p.teaser{
  color: purple;
  }
```

In this CSS, every paragraph that doesn't have a class attribute of teaser will remain black. But those paragraphs with a class attribute of teaser will turn purple, since p.teaser is more specific than p by itself.

Now let's write a rule that's even more specific:

```
p{
  color: black;
  }

p.teaser{
  color: purple;
  }

div#content p.teaser{
  color: orange;
  }
```

Here we're telling any paragraph with a class attribute of teaser that is also inside a <div> tag with an id attribute of content to be orange.

Thinking Beyond Visual Design

Download the video clips for this book from **www.peachpit.com/ cssforprintdesigners** (Register at the site.)

The Internet is an amazing tool for keeping people connected to one another. When it comes to making Web sites, Web designers hold in their hands the ability to make the Internet more enjoyable for everyone.

My hope is that as you start coding Web sites by hand, you continue to learn more about CSS as a craft—as well as a way to make peoples' lives better, even if only by a little bit.

9

Starting from Scratch

Copying and Pasting Repeated Elements for Each Project

NOT EVERYTHING IN print design is terribly creative. Don't get me wrong—some of the things we get to work on are exciting and innovative and highly rewarding. But we spend a lot of time performing repetitive or mundane tasks like flowing 80 pages of text for an annual report; sure, the cover is fun, and maybe even the first ten pages. But the last 70 are, well, work.

I wish I could tell you these types of tasks don't exist in Web design, but the truth is they do, especially when it comes time to start a new project. There's HTML you have to write over and over again for almost every project you work on. That's why I say you should copy and paste it when you start a new project.

Copying and Pasting Saves Time

As a beginning Web coder, it's not important to get very deep into what every line of code means. All you need to know is that there's a bunch of code you need to put at the top of your HTML to make it a valid HTML file. I'll show you where in the code you need to make adjustments so that your code works on your Web site.

WE'RE GOING TO FLY THROUGH THIS SECTION

In my workshops, I cover this topic in about 60 seconds by waving my hand over about 20 lines of dense HTML on a projector screen and telling the print designers, "You don't need to worry about what any of this means—just copy and paste this stuff."

More HTML Tags

TIP You can download these code samples at cssforprintdesigners.com/copy-and-paste.

So far in this book, we've been looking at HTML tags like <div>, <p>, <h1>, and so on. But there are a handful of other tags that don't really have anything to do with the content of a Web site—they're just required for every site we make and they do things like help with search-engine optimization (SEO) and identify which CSS file to use.

These tags mostly go at the very beginning of an HTML file in a <head> tag—but a couple of them (the <html> tag and the <body> tag, to be precise) even wrap all the HTML you write on your own (FIGURE 9.1).

FIGURE 9.1 This is the entire structure of a real HTML document, other than what you need to write from scratch every time.

Let's dig in and take a look at what it takes to make a proper HTML file. First, you need to save a text file with the .html extension. Then, inside of that file, put the following code:

```
<!DOCTYPE html>
<html>
  <head>
    <meta http-equiv="Content-Type" content="text/html; charset=utf-8"/>
    <title>Page Title</title>
    <meta name="description" content="Web site description" />
    <meta name="keywords" content="SEO keywords " />
    <link href="css/screen.css" rel="stylesheet" type="text/css"
    ➥ media="screen" />
    <link href="css/print.css" rel="stylesheet" type="text/css"
    ➥ media="print" />
    <link href="favicon.ico" rel="shortcut icon" type="image/ico" />
  </head>
  <body>
    This is where you put the HTML that you write
  </body>
</html>
```

I've highlighted the parts of this HTML you need to concern yourself with. Simply adjust the values of these attributes for your own Web site and you're good to go.

Page Title

The page title is what shows up in the top of a browser window or tab to identify the Web page (FIGURE 9.2).

FIGURE 9.2 Page titles in our HTML help to identify what each tab is for.

Web Site Description

The Web site description is what search engines show in the preview of search results. Keep it short, no more than a sentence or two.

SEO Keywords

This comma-separated string of characters is part of what search engines look at when determining your site's relevance. Don't use more than 20 or so keywords and keyword phrases, and try not to repeat the same word more than three times.

CSS File

We call CSS with the <link> tag. The path inside the href attribute should lead to a CSS file, which is a text file that ends with the .css extension.

In this example, we have two CSS files. They are both in the css folder, and the files are named screen.css and print.css respectively. You can link to as many CSS files as you want by adding more <link> tags with these attributes.

CSS Media Attribute

The two <link> tags call different CSS files: one for screen viewing and one for printing on paper. The media attribute tells the browser whether to use the CSS file for the screen or for print.

Favicon

A favicon is a small graphic file (16 pixels by 16 pixels in size) that goes in the address bar, tab, or bookmarks bar for your Web site. The file should be saved as a .ico file type. The file should be in the root of your Web site and named favicon.ico.

The <body> Tag

The <body> tag is where you put all of the CSS you write yourself. When I give examples throughout this book, I type something like this:

```
<div id="content">
  <div class="main">
    Main content area
  </div>
  <div class="side">
    Sidebar area
```

```
    </div>
  </div>
```

In a functioning Web site, that code would need to be inside the <body> tag, like this, to work in a real environment:

```
<!DOCTYPE html>
<html>
  <head>
    <meta http-equiv="Content-Type" content="text/html; charset=utf-8"/>
    <title>Page Title</title>
    <meta name="description" content="Web site description" />
    <meta name="keywords" content="SEO keywords " />
    <link href="css/screen.css" rel="stylesheet" type="text/css"
    ➥ media="screen" />
    <link href="favicon.ico" rel="shortcut icon" type="image/ico" />
  </head>
  <body>
    <div id="content">
      <div class="main">
        Main content area
      </div>
      <div class="side">
        Sidebar area
      </div>
    </div>
  </body>
</html>
```

The HTML Framework

In 2009, when I started leading my workshops, I developed and released The HTML Framework (htmlframework.com), a free set of starting files to help Web designers spend less time setting up their HTML files and CSS layouts and more time designing with CSS.

I think this framework is a great starting place for rookies and seasoned Web designers alike because it saves time and prevents some silly typing mistakes.

And trust me, silly typing mistakes are common in the Web-coding world. We can use all the help we can get.

Download the video clips for this book from **www.peachpit.com/ cssforprintdesigners** (Register at the site.)

10

Prepress for the Web

Slicing and Dicing Images so They
Load Fast and Look Good

PREPRESS WORK IS an art that takes patience and experience. To make a design look good when it comes off the press, print designers need to understand the way designs are produced after the files leave the hard drive. This means being familiar with the equipment that produces the plates, the inks that will be used, and the machinery that ultimately spits out digital files and makes them real.

Prepress work also requires a comprehensive understanding of the realities and limitations of the way a piece will be printed—whether it's a gig poster with a short run on a screen press, a print ad that runs on an ancient web press for a local newspaper, or an editorial layout in a glossy magazine that's printed in multiple facilities across the country and distributed to hundreds of thousands of subscribers.

Image Production for Web Design

Web designers have to prep their designs for a production environment, too. But the Web's production environment is all about file size and download speed. On big Web sites with lots of traffic, image size can even have a cost factor.

I'm certain you're used to seeing Web sites with poorly optimized images— which might make you think image production for the Web means you have to save images at a low quality to make them load fast. This might seem frustrating and leave you asking, "Why did I spend so much time making everything look nice in my design if the coder's just going to save it down and make it look cruddy?"

You shouldn't feel that way, because with the right tools and a little patience you don't have to compromise on quality to ensure that your images come out crisp and load fast.

There are a couple of questions that often come up in my workshops: "With all of the image file formats, how do I know which one's the best?" And, "How small should the file size be?"

In this chapter I'm going to demystify image production for the Web and give you the confidence and knowledge you need to start slicing and dicing images that load fast *and* look good.

Starting by Planning

The first step of image production for the Web is to take a good look at your design and figure out which images need to be cut up and pieced together to make the design work. I do this by visualizing two layers of my HTML: the layout and the content. After that, it becomes clear which graphics need to be extracted from the design.

For this chapter, we'll be looking at a sample Web site that has all the elements of a typical Web site (**FIGURE 10.1**).

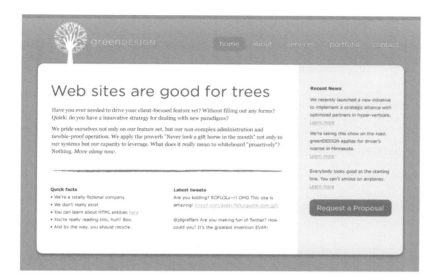

FIGURE 10.1
Our environmentally
friendly Web site.

Start with the Layout

When I start a project, the first thing I do is visualize the layout with boxes. Which tags do I need to accomplish my layout? Which tags should float and in which direction? What order should they be in? Let's take a look at our sample Web design with HTML boxes overlaying it (FIGURE 10.2).

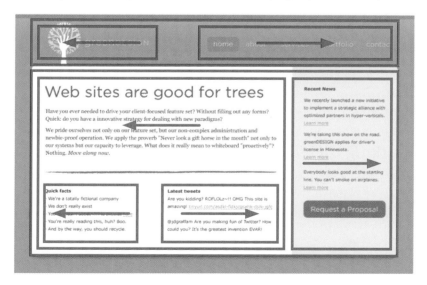

FIGURE 10.2 It helps
to start by visualizing the
layout and floats.

Figuring Out the Layout

Figure 10.2 shows six nested boxes with arrows showing our floats.

In the header area, we have two main containers: one for the logo and one for the site's navigation.

In the content area, we have a main column for content with two smaller columns of text below it. Beside the main content area, we have a sidebar.

Identify the Chunks of Content

After I've identified the major components and can see what HTML is needed to accomplish my layout, I identify all the content that needs to go in each section or module (FIGURE 10.3). This helps me write the rest of my HTML and plan my CSS.

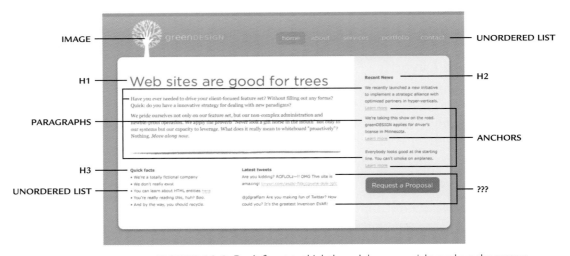

FIGURE 10.3 Don't forget to think through how you might mark up the content.

Marking Up HTML Is Not a Science

Figure 10.3 shows where I'm identifying most of the HTML tags that will need to be written to identify the content of the Web page. I've left some things out, to keep it simple. For example, you know that an unordered list has list items nested inside, and the navigation will have <a> tags inside of each <li> tag.

I've even marked the Latest Tweets section with question marks—that's because sometimes which HTML to use is not clear. In a real-world scenario you may not have any control over these tweets because they might be coming in from a third party. But even if you do have control over the markup, it's difficult to know which HTML tag is best to use. Are they paragraphs? Or is this a list of tweets? Should we just use <div> tags if they're not really paragraphs or a list?

Decide What Images Are Required

Finally, let's overlay some boxes on our design to look at what images are required to make the layout work (**FIGURE 10.4**). We'll be looking at CSS images and content images—remember, content images are what we call with HTML using the <img> tag; decorative images are what we call with CSS using the background property.

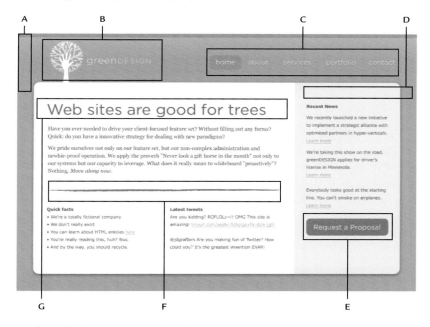

FIGURE 10.4 Zero in on the images you need to export to make the design work. Pay attention to the details.

Look at the design closely—details matter.

A. Notice how we have a subtle gradient across the top of the page, with a darker border at the top. We can repeat the section I have high-lighted on the x-axis to create this effect.

B. This image is the logo, so it's different from the rest—it's considered page content. We'll bring it into our design with HTML using the <img> tag, not CSS.

C. The navigation bar will be a large sprite with hover states. It uses Gotham, a font most users won't have installed on their computers, so we'll also use the image replacement technique we learned about in Chapter 7 to keep the text from overlaying the background image. We'll also need to remember to include the hover effect for each menu item when we make the sprite.

D. To create the fake column that extends all the way down the page vertically on the right, we can cut out this gray bar and repeat it on the y-axis.

E. Like the navigation elements above, this button will be a sprite and we'll use image replacement. We'll need to make sure to remember to design a rollover state.

F. The stroke that divides the main content from the two small columns beneath it can be a background image.

G. This headline uses Gotham, so we'll use image replacement to bring it in as a background image on the <h1> tag.

Understanding Image Formats

Instead of saving everything as a 20-megabyte TIF file as we do for print projects, we need to save our files in formats that have smaller file sizes so they load fast on the Web. There are three formats that are widely used by Web designers: GIF, JPEG, and PNG. Each is good for certain types of images. The way to decide which file format works best is to try all three and see which one produces the best balance of file size and image quality.

The Trusty GIF

The little GIF file format is my favorite, because it gives me the most control over file size. It supports transparency, too, which means it can be great for overlaying on top of a background color or creating subtle texture.

It has limitations though. It supports only 256 colors, which means it's usually not good for photographs. And it has only one level of transparency; each pixel in a GIF is either transparent or opaque. This single-level transparency can lead to graphics with cruddy borders.

The GIF is a great format for graphics like logos, simple illustrations, and gradients that don't have a lot of color variation.

Optimizing GIFs

The GIF file format supports up to 256 colors, but that doesn't mean you need to use all of them. When you go into Photoshop and choose File > Save for Web & Devices and then select GIF from the drop-down list, there will be a little area on the right showing a color table. This color table lists all the colors your graphic uses.

Try reducing the number of colors in the Color option and watching the results live in the left panel under the Optimized tab. When you have made the number of colors as low as possible without sacrificing image quality, you can see how big your file is (**FIGURE 10.5**).

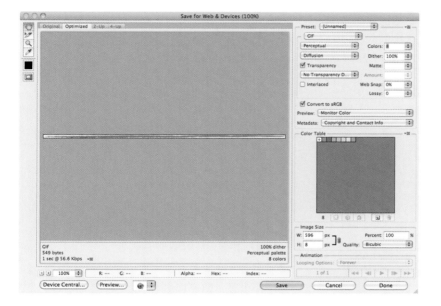

FIGURE 10.5
Pay attention to file size (which appears at the bottom left of this Photoshop dialog) when exporting a GIF. The fewer colors you have, the smaller the file size will be. This one comes in well under 1 KB.

General Rules for GIFs

I know from experience what typically works when optimizing GIF files, so I want to give you a few shortcuts. Remember, I'm speaking in general terms here because your projects will always be different. The best way to learn what works is to try something and see what happens.

- A small GIF image (say, 100 by 20 pixels) should come in under 1 KB.

- A larger GIF image (say, 300 pixels squared) should not be more than 20 KB or so.

- A two-color graphic should be fine with eight colors.

- GIFs *sometimes* work for photography or larger textures, if the image is intentionally grungy. A JPEG image is typically a better choice for photography, though.

Getting Rid of That Cruddy Outline on GIFs

There's a feature in Photoshop's Save for Web & Devices dialog box called Matte that always goes over well in my workshops. I'm always surprised by how many print designers have never heard of this feature of Photoshop. But then again, I guess I shouldn't be surprised. It has no practical use for print designers. And it's on the Save for Web & Devices panel. A print designer would have no reason to go exploring there.

When you choose File > Save for Web & Devices in Photoshop and select GIF from the drop-down list, you'll see an option on the right side labeled Matte. If you have transparency in your GIF, selecting Matte will give you some options for selecting a color to use as a matte color for the edges of your GIF image (FIGURE 10.6).

FIGURE 10.6
The Matte feature in Photoshop's Save for Web & Devices dialog box helps transparent GIFs match up with the background color.

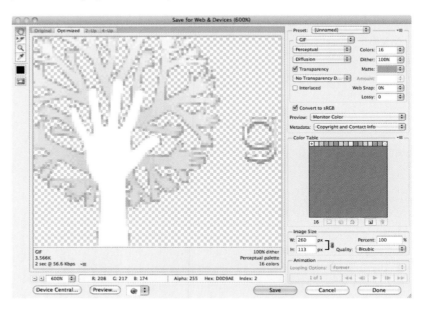

You will want to choose the background color behind your transparent GIF image. Photoshop will then put a horrible-looking, jagged border around the edges of your GIF image that has transparent pixels beside it.

But don't worry—that's what you want. Because if you take that graphic and lay it on top of the color you selected in your Matte settings, something magical happens. Photoshop has blended the edges of your graphic with the matte color and now it looks seamless, just like in our design.

Be careful, though, because you can set only one matte color. A GIF image with a matte color can look great when it matches the background color, but if the background color doesn't match, it won't look good at all.

The All-Mighty JPEG

JPEGs are good for images that have a lot of colors, like photography.

We control a JPEG's file size by adjusting the overall quality of the image by entering a percentage in Photoshop's Save for Web & Devices dialog box (FIGURE 10.7).

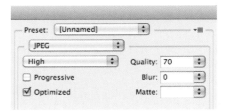

FIGURE 10.7 Adjust the quality and file size of a JPEG in Photoshop's Save for Web & Devices dialog box.

TIP Don't confuse the Save for Web & Devices JPEG settings with the JPEG saving options you get in Photoshop's regular File > Save As dialog box. Save for Web & Devices gives you much greater control over your JPEG quality.

Typically, the human eye can't tell a difference in quality until the quality gets down to about 65 or 70 percent. The lower the percentage, the junkier your JPEG image will look, but the smaller the file size will be.

JPEGs that aren't saved with a high enough quality setting will begin to show something called *artifacting*, which will usually be apparent where one color transitions to another.

The Last-Resort PNG

PNGs are great at maintaining the quality of an image, and they do a pretty decent job of keeping file size down. They also support 256 levels of transparency, which is much better than the GIF. If you have images with rounded corners or drop shadows embedded in them, and you don't know what background color they will sit on, or whether they will show up on different background colors, the PNG format can be a lifesaver.

TWO TYPES OF PNG FORMAT

There are two types of PNG formats to pick from: PNG-8 and PNG-24. PNG-24 is the one that supports full transparency. I rarely use PNG-8 because the results are typically the same as using a GIF. When I talk about PNGs, I'm talking about PNG-24.

TIP **TIP** Internet Explorer 6 does not support PNG transparency. If you're designing a Web site that requires IE6 support, Godspeed—and try to use GIFs whenever possible. There are some workarounds that use JavaScript, but I avoid them whenever possible. You should Google "IE6 PNG fix" if you need to go that route.

We can save graphics as PNGs by going into Photoshop's Save for Web & Devices dialog box and choosing PNG-24.

The problem with PNGs is that we don't have a lot of control over their file size or quality settings (**FIGURE 10.8**), which is why I use PNGs as a last resort when the quality I want cannot be achieved with a GIF or JPEG image. Occasionally a PNG will surprise me and come in with a smaller file size than a GIF or JPEG, but it's a rare occurrence.

FIGURE 10.8 There aren't any options for controlling the file size of a PNG image.

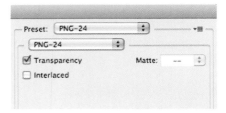

Saving Your Images

Now that we've identified which images we need for our design to work and we have a better understanding of the file types, you can fire up Photoshop and start exporting the images (**FIGURE 10.9**).

FIGURE 10.9 Now that we've extracted all the images from the design, we can start piecing them together using CSS.

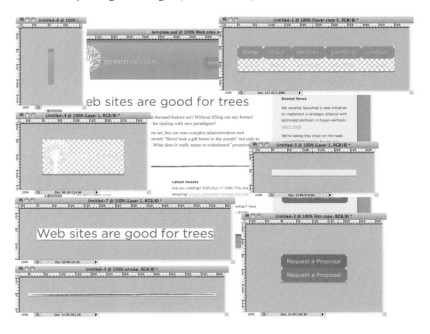

When you're done, you should keep your CSS and HTML images separate from each other. This helps keep your files organized, but it also makes it much easier to type relative paths when coding CSS. For example, `i/graphic.gif` is easier to type than `../css/i/graphic.gif`.

Save the CSS images into a folder specifically for CSS images. Previously, I suggested putting them in `css/i/`.

Web designers typically put HTML images in a folder called `images` or `img`. By now I'm sure you know my vote is for the shorter name.

Measure Twice, Slice Once

The best advice I can give when it comes to image production for the Web is to plan, plan, and plan some more.

You'll save yourself a lot of grief by making your Photoshop comps nice and orderly before you start slicing images. It really is worth the extra time in your design process to name your layers clearly and group them logically.

Download the video clips for this book from **www.peachpit.com/ cssforprintdesigners** (Register at the site.)

> ### DON'T WORK FROM THE ORIGINAL PSD FILE
>
> I'm embarrassed to admit this, but more than once I've been in a hurry and have flattened a gorgeous Photoshop design without saving it, losing the ability to edit the original. D'oh!
>
> My advice? Don't work from the original PSD file when you're slicing and dicing—you might wind up like me, working all night to rebuild the file, crazy layer effects and all.

Also, since we're working with pixels, not vectors, turn on Photoshop's Snap to Pixels feature (FIGURE 10.10). This will keep your shapes aligned on the pixel grid and will prevent fuzzy edges in your final graphics (FIGURE 10.11). It also makes measuring easier.

FIGURE 10.10 Photoshop's Snap to Pixels feature is a time saver. Use it.

FIGURE 10.11 The left side shows what a graphic should look like when your pixels are aligned properly—it will come out looking crisp. The right side, when viewed at 100 percent, will look fuzzy.

Finally, take your time. Don't rush through this critical stage. Try different file formats to see what produces the smallest file size and the highest image quality.

And don't stress if you don't get it perfect the first time—while mistakes in prepress for print design can lead to costly reprints, the Web is forgiving. If you take something live with a less-than-ideal graphic, you can always come back and fix it later.

11

Tools of the Trade

A Quick Guide to the Software You Need for Web Design

EVERY CRAFT HAS a toolset. That's why art school is so expensive. Each class requires different tools—$200 worth of pencils and charcoal for drawing; $400 worth of brushes, paint, canvas, wood, and staples for painting; and $600 worth of film, lenses, and chemicals for photography.

Print designers have tools, too. In addition to software like InDesign, Illustrator, and Photoshop, our desks are cluttered with X-Acto knives, spray adhesive, loupes, and other implements of creation. There's no way around it—we'll need these tools eventually.

Web Design Doesn't Require Many Tools

You don't need expensive software to transition from a print designer to a Web designer—at least, not yet. Maybe later, when you're marking up complex layouts and coding CSS in your sleep. For now, I want you to focus on the basics.

Those basics are

- The software you already have
- A text editor
- A few plug-ins for your Web browser

Yep. That's it. You can become a Web designer without forking out much extra cash, if any at all.

The Web Designer's Toolbox

Before you start making a Web site, you need to know what tools are out there. I'm not providing a comprehensive list here—I'm just giving you places to start looking. I'm keeping the list intentionally short and focusing only on what you need to get started.

As you work more and more on Web design projects, you'll find great tools that I haven't listed here—even some I haven't heard of. Just remember, when it comes down to it, it's what you do with the tools, not the tools themselves.

Photoshop (or Fireworks)

I said this previously, but it's worth reiterating here: Photoshop is not the only application for designing Web sites. A lot of Web designers will tell you Fireworks is the way to go, and they have some good points. But I'm more familiar with Photoshop, and you probably are, too. Plus, you probably already own a copy of Photoshop.

WHAT ABOUT DESIGNING WITH ILLUSTRATOR?

I have designed in Illustrator a couple of times, but have stayed away from it recently. Illustrator does have a pixel view, which can be helpful for Web design projects, but overall it's optimized for vector graphics. Plus, I always have a much easier time exporting graphics with Photoshop than with Illustrator.

Use the program you're more comfortable with to get your overall concept down, but my recommendation is to finish everything in Photoshop.

FTP

We learned about FTP in Chapter 3. Odds are, at some point, you've used FTP to upload large files for a print job rather than burning and shipping a disc.

When we're done building our Web site on our computer, we need to upload it to a Web server to make the site live. That's where FTP comes in. If you don't have an FTP application already, here are some of my favorites.

For Mac users

- Panic's Transmit ($35, at panic.com/transmit)
- Fetch ($30, at fetchsoftworks.com)
- Cyberduck (free, at cyberduck.ch)

For Windows users

- SmartFTP ($40, at smartftp.com)
- CoffeeCup's Free FTP (free, at coffeecup.com/free-ftp/)

Text Editor

Everything we've learned in this book has involved typing text. And no, we don't type code in Microsoft Word. We type it in a plain text editor.

For Mac users

- TextWrangler (free, at barebones.com/products/TextWrangler/)
- BBEdit ($100, at barebones.com/products/bbedit/)
- Panic's Coda ($100, at panic.com/coda/)

For Windows users

- CoffeeCup's Free HTML Editor (free, at coffeecup.com/free-editor/)
- CoffeeCup's The HTML Editor ($50, at coffeecup.com/html-editor/)
- Notepad++ (free, at notepad-plus-plus.org)

 TIP A lot of print designers already have a copy of Dreamweaver. Contrary to what many Web coders may say, it's not a bad text editor. If you have it, use it. If not, don't feel compelled to fork out the cash to get it—there are other, less expensive options.

SAVE HTML AND CSS FILES WITH THE RIGHT FILE EXTENSIONS

When you're using a plain text editor and you go to save your file, you have the option to decide what file extension to use. In case you didn't know, when you're making HTML files, you need to save the files with the .html extension. When you're making CSS files, you need to save the files with the .css extension.

Browsers and Plug-ins

As you know, there are several Web browsers to choose from these days—and they're all pretty good. When you start coding Web pages from scratch, it's a good idea to download all of the major browsers and have them all handy to make sure your Web page looks good in each of them.

But you need to pick a browser to use when building your Web site. Firefox is my go-to browser when developing sites because it has a lively community of developers who have built plug-ins that make coding much easier.

Here are a couple of my favorite plug-ins.

Firebug

Firebug (addons.mozilla.org/en-US/firefox/addon/firebug/) is a Web development tool that extends Firefox by letting you inspect the HTML and CSS of a Web page (FIGURE 11.1).

FIGURE 11.1 Firebug saves Web developers a lot of time by giving them a visual way to browse a Web page's code.

Firebug is good for troubleshooting your own code, but it can be especially helpful if want to look at someone else's Web site to see how that person accomplished a treatment with CSS. It shows you the HTML and CSS that applies just to that element so you don't have to go swimming through hundreds or thousands of lines of code to piece together what's happening.

MeasureIt

MeasureIt (addons.mozilla.org/en-US/firefox/addon/measureit/) is a handy little tool for measuring anything on your Web page (FIGURE 11.2).

FIGURE 11.2
MeasureIt makes it easy to take measurements on a Web page.

Putting It All Together

Now you know everything you need to know to make a Web site on your own. We've covered everything: screen sizes, paths, HTML, CSS layout, CSS3, accessibility, image production, and the tools of the trade.

All you have to do now is get to work.

Download the video clips for this book from **www.peachpit.com/ cssforprintdesigners** (Register at the site.)

12

Any Questions?

A Collection of Real Questions from Real Print Designers

WHEN I LEAD my workshops, I make sure to gear my presentation toward beginners—I want to avoid using technical jargon that means something in the Web design community but doesn't mean anything to print designers.

The way I teach HTML and CSS to print designers is basic: You need to know HTML; HTML is made up of tags; a tag looks like this; now, here's what CSS looks like and some tips and tricks on how to use it.

See? I just put the entire book in a compound sentence.

Since it's such a simple way of talking about hand coding, the attendees start raising their hands halfway through the workshop and asking some pretty advanced questions. I'm always impressed by the quality of the questions.

I reserved this chapter of the book to address those questions. These are the real questions I have been asked over several years of leading my CSS for Print Designers workshops.

Frequently Asked Questions

These questions range from basic to advanced. I won't go into great detail in my answers. Instead, I'm going to give you enough information to understand the basic concept and then you can go to Google to figure out the rest.

Which Web sites are good resources?

The World Wide Web Consortium (w3.org) tells you the proper way to code Web sites, though the site is pretty technical. Go there when you're looking for the technical definition of something, or when you're trying to fall asleep.

A List Apart (alistapart.com) is an online magazine that publishes a couple of new articles every two weeks. The topics are sometimes for advanced coders, but often resonate with beginners as well. The writing is always superb, and the thinking is always progressive.

Chris Coyier's CSS Tricks (css-tricks.com) is a Web design community. Chris is always posting inventive ways to accomplish things with CSS. He also writes in a way that's easy to understand.

Smashing Magazine (smashingmagazine.com) belongs in this list simply because of the volume of articles this magazine puts out. It's not exclusive to Web design, because it also posts articles on print design. I check in here a couple times each week.

The Photoshop Etiquette Manifesto for Web Designers (photoshopetiquette.com) is a list of helpful and subtle suggestions for organizing Photoshop documents, making transfer of them less painful. Read this—it's essential for staying organized.

There are thousands of great Web design blogs and resources out there—I couldn't possibly list them all. Beyond these, I suggest following Web designers on Twitter to see what they're talking about and linking to.

I've heard you can use only one <h1> tag per page for SEO. Is that true?

Remember how I told you there's new HTML and old HTML? Well, the newer version, HTML5, doesn't care how many <h1> tags you have, as long as you only have one <h1> tag per *container*. With HTML4, you're supposed to have only one <h1> tag per *page*.

To make sure you're using HTML5, use the DOCTYPE you learned about in Chapter 9. If your document doesn't have the HTML5 DOCTYPE listed here, you can only use one <h1> tag per page:

```
<!DOCTYPE html>
```

HTML4 DOCTYPES

Other, older DOCTYPES will look a lot more complicated than the HTML5 DOCTYPE. Here are a few you might come across. Notice they're only slightly different from each other, but they're all way more complicated than the HTML5 DOCTYPE:

```
<!DOCTYPE HTML PUBLIC "-//W3C//DTD HTML 4.01//EN"
"http://www.w3.org/TR/html4/strict.dtd">
```

```
<!DOCTYPE HTML PUBLIC "-//W3C//DTD HTML 4.01 Transitional//EN"
"http://www.w3.org/TR/html4/loose.dtd">
```

```
<!DOCTYPE html PUBLIC "-//W3C//DTD XHTML 1.0 Strict//EN"
"http://www.w3.org/TR/xhtml1/DTD/xhtml1-strict.dtd">
```

See? You don't want to learn that, do you?

What's wrong with using tables for layout?

When you use tables for layout, you're not properly identifying the content. Content needs to be properly identified to make it easier to maintain and more reusable.

Fifteen years ago while I was mourning the loss of Kurt Cobain, Web coders were thinking up inventive ways to mimic print design on the screen. Web browsers sucked back then, even more than IE6. They couldn't handle floats, and CSS was just a little bitty baby.

Anyway, coders at that time figured out that by using the <table> tag, along with table rows (the <tr> tag) and table data cells (the <td> tag), they could create more complex layouts, just like in the print design world. It worked, but it sacrificed meaning.

Fast-forward to today. We don't need no stinkin' tables. We have good browsers.

Is there a proper time to use tables when coding Web sites?

Absolutely. When your content is made up of tabular data, you *should* use tables to flow the content. Tables can get pretty complex, so I don't cover them in my workshops, and I left them out of this book.

If you want to learn more about how to make proper tables with HTML, you can Google "HTML table." Remember, HTML tables are just made up of tags, so you can hook into them with CSS to make them more attractive.

How should we design for the "fold" when we design Web sites?

The fold is a figment of your imagination. It's a concept from print design (newspapers, to be precise) based on a fixed height. The Web, as you know, doesn't have a fixed height.

But we still have to deal with the fact that your Web content will be cut off at different heights by different peoples' screens. We may not know where exactly, but we can make a pretty good guess as to the range of where it might be.

TIP The scroll bar in the browser is not enough. Users don't pay attention to it until they realize they need it.

This imaginary "fold" is typically 500–700 pixels from the top of the page. I design around it by making sure my design has something that starts and ends outside that range (FIGURE 12.1).

Web designers don't need to try and make everything on the homepage fit "above the fold." Instead, we need to design so that there's some indication that there's more content below.

FIGURE 12.1 Instead of cramming everything above the fold, just give users an indication there's something below it.

THE FOLD IS SOMEWHERE IN THIS AREA.

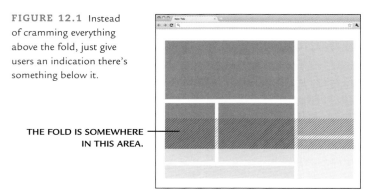

What is div-based layout? Is that the same as CSS layout?

Yes. When someone says "div layout" they mean CSS layout. Don't forget that there are other tags besides <div> tags that can be used for layout.

With HTML5 we now have <header>, <section>, <article>, <aside>, <footer>, and more. As a general rule, I called it CSS layout.

How do you deal with IE6?

First, my firm doesn't support IE6 without charging extra. It's a really old browser and hardly anyone uses it any more. Plus, most of the really frustrating bugs come from IE6 and it can take quite some time to figure them out. Dealing with IE6 is not child's play.

Sometimes, though, IE6 support is a requirement. Some of the most frustrating and bizarre IE6 bugs and simple workarounds are listed here:

- Depending which DOCTYPE you're using, IE6 may not calculate the width of an object with padding or borders correctly. I avoid putting padding and border on the left and right sides of tags that are used for layout to sidestep this problem. You can learn more than you need to know if you Google "IE6 box model."

- When something is floated in IE6, don't put a margin on the right side of it. If you do, that right margin's value will double. You can learn more if you Google "IE6 double margin."

- When you float objects in IE6, make sure the parent container has line-height: 0; to make sure each tag aligns horizontally. Google "stepdown bug" to learn more.

How do we make special characters like em dashes, curly quotes, and such?

It's best not to copy and paste special characters into your HTML, because text has to be encoded properly to work on every computer. Instead, you'll need to learn about HTML character entities. They look funny, and you've probably seen them before.

Basically, an HTML character entity is made up of an ampersand and a semi-colon with some sort of number or text string inside. You just type the entity, and the browser renders the proper character.

TABLE 12.1 gives you some of the most common HTML character entities.

TABLE 12.1 Common HTML Character Entities

ENTITY	WHAT IT LOOKS LIKE	ENTITY	WHAT IT LOOKS LIKE
©	©	“	"
™	™	”	"
‘	'	—	—
’	'	–	–

Is there a way to check our code to make sure we're doing it right?

Yes, HTML and CSS can be checked automatically to see if they follow all the rules. I use the W3C's Validator (validator.w3.org) to check my code. If you have a layout that doesn't look right, check to make sure your code is valid. Fixing errors will usually fix something you think should work.

But remember, just because your code is valid doesn't mean it's good. Good HTML properly identifies the content it surrounds, is formatted cleanly, and has class and id attributes that don't imply how something should look.

What books do you recommend?

After this book, I recommend *Designing with Web Standards, Third Edition* by Jeffrey Zeldman and *Bulletproof Web Design, Second Edition* by Dan Cederholm.

Coding Is an Art

Print designers work in communication, advertising, and marketing. They're online all day. They even help plan and execute online marketing strategies for clients and read blog posts about "user experience." Furthermore, almost every single print designer out there has, at some point, designed something for the Web. Knowing about the Web is just part of the job.

Regardless of this level of familiarity with Web technologies, the thought of coding something by hand makes some print designers break out into a sweat. That's because print designers have never been taught code in a visual way, so it hasn't made sense to them.

There are just so many questions: Can I do this? Should I do that? How would you make these? If I try this, will my design break? Can I fix it if it breaks?

Every question about coding has one source—print designers are scared of doing it the "wrong way." Every single step of the process is daunting, intimidating, unknown. But learning to code shouldn't be that way.

There Is No Wrong Way to Learn

Coding is art. And just like art, you have to experiment with it to see what works and what doesn't. Think of HTML and CSS as materials like clay, and you want to make a clay bowl for your mom. How nice!

There are tools and techniques for spinning clay into a beautiful bowl. And those tools and techniques take practice. You can read up on and research the tools until you know everything there is to know about them. And I'd still bet money that the first time you sit down to spin clay, regardless of your research and planning, you make a mess.

That's OK; it's even the point. Coding should be fun to learn. When you try something new that you think might work, and it actually works, your face will light up with joy at your creation.

I want you to make a mess with code. Play with it, have fun, get your hands dirty.

INDEX